The British Court

By the Same Author

SPLENDID OCCASIONS IN ENGLISH HISTORY, 1520–1947

Her Majesty the Queen on her way to open Parliament, November 1952

IFAN KYRLE FLETCHER

THE BRITISH COURT

Its Traditions and Ceremonial

with 22 half-tone illustrations

CASSELL & COMPANY LTD

LONDON

CASSELL & CO LTD

37/38 St. Andrew's Hill, Queen Victoria Street
London, E.C. 4

and at

210 Queen Street, Melbourne
26/30 Clarence Street, Sydney
P.O. Box 9, Lower Hutt, N.Z.
1068 Broadview Avenue, Toronto 6
122 East 55th Street, New York 22
Avenida 9 de Julho 1138, São Paulo
Galeria Güemes, Escritorio 518/520
Florida 165, Buenos Aires
Haroon Chambers, South Napier Road, Karachi
15 Graham Road, Ballard Estate, Bombay 1
17 Central Avenue P.O. Dharamtala, Calcutta
P.O. Box 275, Cape Town
P.O. Box 1386, Salisbury, S. Rhodesia
P.O. Box 959, Accra, Gold Coast
Calcada Do Carma 55–2°, Lisbon
25 rue Henri Barbusse, Paris 5e
Islands Brygge 5, Copenhagen

First published April 1953

*Set in 11pt. Bembo type and
printed in Great Britain by
Wyman & Sons, Ltd., London, Fakenham and Reading*
F.153

Contents

Illustrations

vi

ILLUSTRATIONS

The photographs in this book are reproduced by permission of the following copyright owners:

Barrat's Photo Press Ltd: Frontispiece. British Museum: 8, 9, 15. Central Press Photos Ltd: 4, 10, 12, 18. Crown Copyright: 14. Fox Photos Ltd: 5. Keystone Press Ltd: 19. P.A.—Reuter Photos Ltd: 13, 16, 20, 21. Pix Photos Ltd: 1. Topical Press Agency Ltd: 2, 3, 6, 7.

ACKNOWLEDGMENTS

I WISH to express my sense of indebtedness to all those who have placed their expert knowledge at my disposal in the writing of this book. My gratitude for being allowed to share in the fruits of their erudition is increased by my knowledge of the patience and generosity with which they have answered my inquiries. I am specially mindful of the assistance I have received from Ernest Barry, Esq., the Queen's Barge Master; Richard Buckle, Esq.; the late Sir William Ll. Davies, Librarian of the National Library of Wales; Garter King of Arms; John Hunt, Esq., of the Crown Office; Sir Norman Gwatkin, of the Lord Chamberlain's Office; Captain Iain Moncreiffe; Sir Owen Morshead, the Royal Librarian; G. Noakes, Esq., Assistant Chief of Establishments at the Bank of England; Harold D. Rosenthal, Esq., the Archivist at the Royal Opera House, Covent Garden.

I am grateful to Messrs. John Lane The Bodley Head, Ltd., for permission to quote Sir Max Beerbohm's words about George IV, from *Works*; to Mrs. W. B. Yeats, Macmillan & Co., Ltd., and Messrs. A. P. Watt & Son for permission to quote from *The Collected Poems of W. B. Yeats*; and to John Murray (Publishers) Ltd., for permission to quote from *The Girlhood of Queen Victoria*.

I.K.F.

Introduction

Customs and ceremonial are not easily disentangled from the complex structure of British history. They lie mostly beneath the surface of life, emerging occasionally in forms to which we are now so accustomed, like the games that children play, changing with the seasons and in response to what seems to be traditional knowledge, that, if they are questioned at all, they are soon accepted as part of the essential movement of the ordered life of a community. It is good to think of the ceremonial expressions of celebration as crystallized play, because only so do they remind us immediately of the instinctive nature of events which would otherwise seem artificial. By the museum conservation of folk customs, the debasement of the medieval royal entry into the modern historical pageant and other forms of artificial survival, the distance is increased between our complicated urban life and those simpler periods when every activity of man—his religion, his love, his sense of kingship, his labour and his pleasure—was spontaneously recognized as material proper for a system of royal ceremony.

It is in the little sheltered world around the monarchy that British customs and ceremonial still have authentic roots. Here ceremony is still almost an instinct, nurtured by twelve hundred years of recorded kingly rites and, behind the records, centuries of unwritten traditions. These antique forms and orders, placing a controlling influence upon the Queen and her Court, seem to the casual eye to have little relevance to the world of today, but there are times when they make a vivid impact. First amongst these is the coronation, when, by a sudden dispersal of the mists of time, millions of people may see the clearest image of the activity of a sovereign—his possession of all princely virtues, from which grow the fruits of good works, justice, mercy, the protection, cherishing, and direction of his people. This symbol, a reflection of man's age-old dream of kingship, is vivid to the world for one day in a generation. The truth that it is always present for those who seek it is left to the poet to find when he reminds us of its existence with his question,

> "How but in custom and in ceremony
> Are innocence and beauty born?"

1. *The Monarchy*

ONARCHY is a big word, of good import, of evil import, at different times and in different places. But, whatever else it may have been and still is, it expresses an idea that has always been a necessity from the first organization of human life. Perhaps even the word human is too limiting and it may be that the idea of the unique ruler came to primitive man by communication with other and even more primitive forms of life. But in these senses it is one of the great abstractions which hang as nebulous as clouds across the horizon of our lives. Monarchy, like our friends, must be studied to be understood. We do not begin by asking what our friends mean, in a philosophical sense. We notice what they say, what they do, even how they look, and gradually, over a long spell, we come to have a small conception of what they are. Never more than that, for all essences are incommunicable. By the same instinctive process we may move towards an understanding of a generalization such as the monarchy. It is a process of some value to people who have seen the idea of the leader twisted into obscene and monstrous caricatures. Reassurance may be necessary, not only of the original conception of sovereignty but of our acceptance of it—reassurance that may perhaps be found in the interplay of king and people over a great stretch of recorded history, not in these islands only but in all those places beyond the seas that are called British.

The powers of the British Sovereign have never been closely defined. During the past nine hundred years they have frequently been adjusted or curtailed. It would be possible to say that, as a result of these historical processes, the powers of the Monarch could now be formalized and that they would be found to be slight. Such a statement, if made, would be one of those irrelevant judgments in which, through a failure to count imagination at its proper value, the facts are made to add up to a fragment of their total sum. It is true that the Sovereign's functions of treating with foreign powers, of appointing Ministers, ambassadors, judges, and officers of the armed forces, of creating peers and conferring honours, of summoning and dissolving Parliament, of assenting to legislation, are all for the most part formal. But there is real power in the Sovereign's function of appointing a Prime Minister. The continuity of government rests with the Monarch. The importance of the Monarch's position as the ultimate source of constitutional power is heightened by the fact that Parliament has no voice in the appointment of either the Prime Minister or the Cabinet, and that neither of these essential instruments has statutory existence. The choice of the Premier is often automatic but there have been occasions in living memory when the Sovereign has been called upon to make an important act of personal judgment. The selection of the Cabinet is made at the discretion of the Prime Minister.

Even the formal functions of the Monarch sometimes involve the problems of decision. In 1910 situations arose which proved that the Monarch could and should, in certain circumstances, refuse to create peers for political purposes and refuse to allow a dissolution of Parliament if he believes that it would be an abuse of sound constitutional principles. The Monarch does not attempt to thwart the will of the people but to delay political action long enough to allow that will to be clearly expressed. In so doing he follows the fundamental principle of parliamentary government that the people are ruled by the King in Parliament, that is, by His Majesty's Government checked, opposed, and criticized by His Majesty's Opposition. How recent is this conception will be realized when it is remembered that, at the beginning of her reign, Queen Victoria regarded Her Majesty's Opposition as opposition to Her Majesty.

Beyond these powers lie the great tracts of personal influence. The Sovereign may ask for explanations whenever delegated legislation passes the Privy Council. He may offer advice to his Ministers at any time. He has a staff to keep him informed of political developments and he may seek information in every quarter, even if there is only one Minister whose advice he is constitutionally bound to accept. He is outside politics and removed from the pressure of everyday events, yet no one is nearer to the sources of political power and to the control of those events. His influence must always be at one remove but when it is based upon judgment and character, as to the great benefit of this country it has so often been, its potentialities are without limits. Our conception of the power of that influence may be measured by the recognition that it is no longer metaphorical to say that the British Empire, a complex and varied system of governments and communities, is held together by the constitutional monarchy.

The relationship between the United Kingdom and the Dominions has been the subject of earnest deliberations for at least fifty years. In 1901 by the Royal Titles Act, Edward VII was declared to be King of "the British Dominions beyond the Seas". The term Dominions was here understood to apply in the widest sense to all British territories

overseas, but in 1907 the first of the quadrennial Imperial
Conferences was held in which the constitutional status of
the self-governing Dominions was discussed. A definition
of these self-governing communities was made by the
Conference held in 1926, which included the important
statement that the Dominions are "united by a common
allegiance to the Crown". This was carried further by
the Conference of 1930, as a result of which the Statute of
Westminster was passed by the British Parliament in De-
cember 1931. This constitutional rule gave the Dominions
powers over their own legislation and, by the first paragraph
of the preamble, further strengthened the bond between
the monarchy and the Dominion Parliaments.

And whereas it is meet and proper to set out by way of
preamble to this Act that, inasmuch as the Crown is the
symbol of the free associations of the members of the
British Commonwealth of Nations, and as they are united
by a common allegiance to the Crown, it would be in
accord with the established constitutional position of all
the members of the Commonwealth in relation to one
another that any alteration in the law touching the Succession to the Throne or the Royal Style and Titles shall
hereafter require the assent as well of the Parliaments of
all the Dominions as of the Parliament of the United
Kingdom.

One result of this new relationship was a change in the
status of the Governor-General of each Dominion. He was
no longer the representative of the Government of the
United Kingdom but His Majesty's personal representative, appointed upon the sole and exclusive advice of the
Government of the Dominion concerned. The exact

constitutional relationship that exists between the Monarch and his Ministers in the United Kingdom exists also between the Governor-General and the Dominion Ministers—a relationship which is a delicate balance of conventions and usages achieved by a process of growth in toleration. The oath administered to King George VI in 1937 was a symbol that our monarchy and our constitution have developed side by side since the days of King Alfred. The King took the Saxon oath to execute Law and Justice, in Mercy, and, for the first time, he solemnly promised to govern, according to their respective laws and customs, the people of Great Britain and of each of his Dominions, severally and individually named.

India's desire to become a republic, while remaining within the Commonwealth, and the granting of Dominion status to Ceylon brought the Commonwealth Declaration of 1949, by which the King was recognized as the symbol of the free association of the independent member States of the Commonwealth and as such the Head of the Commonwealth. The King was still the one essential link between the eight great nations. The Commonwealth Conference of 1952 recognized the strength of this link between the diversities of race, religion, language and constitution by recommending that each member country should use for its own purposes a form of title which suits its own particular circumstances but retains a substantial element which is common to all.

Of equal importance with the powers and the personal influence of the Monarch is his position as the symbol of the dignity of the State. The pageantries of kingship, supported and enhanced by the Court and its ceremonial, the coronation, the investitures, the rites of the orders of chivalry, are still alive in our midst. They are accepted as being more than the gilded trappings of outworn majesty. Perhaps in the hearts of the people these ceremonies are recognized, in the Chinese sense, as the outward expression of inward feeling, although the furthest that our prosaic politicians can go is to admit that public opinion today likes a certain amount of pageantry.

The Royal Family had no surname before 1917. The dynasty was called the house of Hanover or more recently the house of Guelph. King George V proclaimed that the descendants of Queen Victoria should be styled and known as the house and family of Windsor, and Queen Elizabeth II has confirmed this declaration. The Queen's own style, by the law existing at her accession, was "Elizabeth the Second, By the Grace of God of Great Britain, Ireland, and of the British Dominions Beyond the Seas, Queen, Defender of the Faith". But, by the Proclamation in Council of February 1952, she was proclaimed as "by the Grace of God, Queen of this Realm and of all her other Realms and Territories, Head of the Commonwealth, Defender of the Faith". The noble title of "Head of the Commonwealth" was accepted by the Commonwealth Conference of 1952 and will be used in the seven different titles by which the Queen will be designated at her Coronation. The style of "Defender of the Faith", the Sovereign's one non-regal title, is bestowed by Parliamentary authority. This ecclesiastical honour was first granted by Pope Leo X to Henry VIII but in the troubles that developed between the Tudor monarch and the Vatican the title was withdrawn. It was then conferred upon the King by Parliament.

The eldest son of the Monarch, the heir apparent, is born Duke of Cornwall in the peerage of England, and Duke of Rothesay, Earl of Carrick, and Baron of Renfrew in the peerage of Scotland. He is immediately entitled to all the rights and revenues belonging to the Duchy of Cornwall.

In spite of this the Civil List for the present reign allows for the revenues to be applied during the minority of the Duke in relief of the Civil List, subject to a prior charge for his maintenance and education. The Dukedom of Cornwall, the first English duchy, was created in 1337 by Edward III for his son, Edward, the Black Prince. The Duke is accepted in law as being of full age at his birth. This means that he could take his seat in the House of Lords at any age, but it is customary to wait until the royal legal age of eighteen. The titles of Prince of Wales and Earl of Chester are not his by right but are conferred by special creation and investiture. When the heir apparent becomes Prince of Wales he also becomes, by the statutes of the Order, a Knight of the Garter.

The second English Dukedom, that of Lancaster, was created in 1351, but with the accession of Edward IV the Duchy was annexed to the Crown in perpetuity. In this way has arisen the strange anomaly that there is a Duchy of Lancaster but no Duke. At the accession of Elizabeth II the new queen was toasted in Lancashire as "The Queen, Duke of Lancaster". This is a harmless example of local patriotism, but the joint title is without legal basis. A Lord Chief Justice has ruled that there is "absolute incapacity of the Sovereign to hold a dignity". The lands and revenues of the Duchy are always vested in the Sovereign and his heirs. The principal official of the Duchy, the Chancellor, is now a member of the Government. The appointment is usually given to a distinguished person whose assistance as a Minister is necessary to the Government but who cannot undertake the duties of a department.

The position of Queens Consort is clearly defined in the British system. They share the King's rank, styles, position, and influence, as they share his coronation. But the status

[17]

of Princes Consort is different, even as a man in other walks of life derives no honour or rank from the position of his wife. There are no special ranks or privileges attached to the husband of a Queen Regnant. The Duke of Edinburgh is the fourth in English history and of his predecessors only Prince Albert was accorded the style of Prince Consort. This title, granted to him by Letters Patent, came seventeen years after his marriage to Queen Victoria.

The eldest daughter of the Sovereign bears the courtesy title of Princess Royal, a practice begun by George II for his daughter, Anne. There was at least one earlier, if isolated, example of the title. Pepys records that it was used by Mary, the eldest daughter of Charles I. The title is conferred for life. This is the reason why it was not borne by the present Queen, as it is still held by her aunt, Princess Mary.

2. Royal Residences

THE royal residences may be divided into six groups
—palaces which are official seats of the Court, such
as Buckingham Palace, St. James's Palace, Windsor
Castle, the Palace of Holyroodhouse; private residences of
the Sovereign—Sandringham, Balmoral Castle, Royal Lodge,
and Frogmore; residences of other members of the Royal
Family—Marlborough House and Clarence House; palaces
which are used partly for museum and partly for residential
purposes, "by grace and favour" of the Monarch, such as
Hampton Court and Kensington Palace; those no longer
used as royal residences—the Tower of London, Osborne,
Whitehall, Greenwich; those which are names and memories
only—a great number, of which Kew and Richmond will
serve as examples.

Buckingham Palace, the principal residence of the Sovereign, is superbly placed at the west end of the Mall, but its
modern exterior is hardly fitted to be the culmination of
the finest processional street in London. The first residence on this site was called Buckingham House, after Queen
Anne's favourite, the Duke of Buckingham. In 1705 this
nobleman, the patron of Dryden and the friend of Pope,
employed Captain Wynne, a Dutch architect, to build a
house for him on the edge of St. James's Park. It was the
most splendid private house in London and its magnificent
double staircase was the admiration of the town. George
III purchased it in 1765 and George IV commissioned Nash

to build a new palace for his personal residence, when his Regency marvel, Carlton House, was being demolished. The extravagance that characterized all this Monarch's schemes caused a halt in the work in 1829. William IV authorized a modest continuation in 1833 and further altera- tions, including the addition of an extra floor for Court offices, were made before Queen Victoria took up residence there in 1837. In spite of these operations lasting twenty years and the young Queen's cheerful comment that she was much pleased with her rooms, the Palace remained almost uninhabitable by modern standards until the Prince Consort organized its improvements. Since 1837 it has been regularly used as the London residence of the Sovereign and the centre of Court ceremonial.

St. James's Palace is a sober group of red-brick buildings. Its ancient importance as a royal residence is reflected in the fact that foreign ambassadors are still accredited to the Court of St. James's. The first building on this site was a hospital for leprous maidens, which was acquired and rebuilt by Henry VIII. Mary I lived here and Elizabeth I stayed here at the time of the Armada crisis. While the Palace of Whitehall was the principal residence of the Stuart monarchs, St. James's was used by the heirs to the throne, first Henry, Prince of Wales, and later his brother, Prince Charles. During these residences many new buildings grew up around the original St. James's House, until it was rightly called "a little town in itself", with a character it still maintains. In 1698, when Whitehall was destroyed by fire, William III made St. James's Palace the official seat of the Court. This it remained until its own fiery destruction in 1809. Relics of the old buildings still remain—the Gateway is part of the house in which Henry VIII lived with Ann Boleyn, the old kitchen built by Vanbrugh in 1716 is now the dining-room of the Queen's Guard, the changing of the Guard takes place on the Colour Court surrounded by the unostentatious buildings that have housed members of the Royal Family for four hundred years.

Windsor Castle is one of the most historic places in Europe. Situated on an eminence above the River Thames, the great castle is built around a fortified mound of extraordinary antiquity. The first stone buildings were erected by William the Conqueror and from his day for nearly nine hundred years the Kings of England have lived within the circuit wall which he commenced to build. Many monarchs have made their contribution to the building. Henry III erected the first Round Tower. Edward III reconstructed it on a greater scale as a meeting-place of the Knights of the Order of the Garter. The Chapel of St. George, now the Royal Mausoleum, is a product of a truly English genius, a masterpiece of the time of Edward IV. Nowhere abroad, and only at King's College, Cambridge and Henry VII's Chapel at Westminster in this country, can the airy grace of this summer noontide church be matched. It is the Royal Chapel—in its choir hang the banners of the Knights of the Garter, in its vaults lie the bodies of Kings of England, from Edward IV who built it to George VI. The State Apartments in the castle were erected in the time of Charles II. Sir Christopher Wren had the intention to restore the whole castle for his Royal master but that task of doubtful value was left, first, to George III who, wishing to make Windsor his home, altered the castle in keeping with the taste of the Gothic revival, and, much more completely, to Sir Jeffrey Wyatville, who transformed it for George IV. Whatever archæological discussions it may arouse there is no doubt that Windsor Castle, seen from the river or, as it used to be seen, from the end of the Long Walk, that superb

[21]

double avenue of elms laid out by Charles II, is one of the most impressive buildings in the country and that it stirs in its beholders a desire to echo Shakespeare's wish

> "That it may stand till the perpetual doom,
> In state as wholesome, as in state 'tis fit."

Windsor has given its name to a most colourful addition to English costume. This is the Windsor Uniform, consisting of a blue coat with red collar and cuffs, and blue or white waistcoat, worn by members of the Royal Family, by royal or other distinguished guests by permission of the Sovereign, and by members of the Royal Household, at dinner while the Court is in residence at Windsor. The idea of a uniform that would link together the Monarch, his family, his intimate friends, and the senior officials of his household was first put into effect by George III, who may have derived it from Germany in emulation of Frederick the Great's personal uniform. There is a tradition that the colours were copied from the livery of the Pembroke family, due to George III's admiration for Lady Pembroke in his youth. Another survival of these colours is the blue and red livery worn by the staff at Burlington House, a relic of the early days of the Royal Academy when it was founded and controlled by George III. The Windsor Uniform was widely used by that addict of fashion, George IV, not only at Windsor but also at Ascot and Brighton. Queen Victoria had an affection for it and insisted that her equerries wore it for many of their daily duties at Windsor, sometimes with black-strapped "overalls" and even with pepper-and-salt trousers. These variations were suppressed by Edward VII, although the sumptuous full-dress form covered with gold braid and the feminine version, worn for riding with a white beaver hat with white feathers, disappeared with the eighteenth century. It survives in its undress form, worn only as evening dress.

The Palace of Holyroodhouse at Edinburgh was originally an abbey founded in 1128. Connected with this is a part of a royal palace erected by the Scottish monarchs, James IV and James V. In this old building are the apartments occupied by Mary, Queen of Scots. Cromwell's soldiers destroyed much of it in 1650 but this great enemy of the Scots commenced the building of a new palace when he became Lord Protector, a work which was continued by Charles II. The loyalty that the people of Scotland had expressed to him by his coronation at Scone in 1654, when he was a fugitive from his country, gave him every cause to express his gratitude. In this new building is the great picture gallery, with over a hundred mythical portraits of Scottish kings, in which the election of representative peers for Scotland takes place. Since the Act of Union of 1707 many British kings have held court within the walls of Holyroodhouse and one of Elizabeth II's first official visits in June 1952 was in continuation of this tradition.

Oldest of the private residences still used by the Sovereign is Royal Lodge in Windsor Great Park. In 1812 John Nash constructed a cottage *ornée* for the Prince Regent. Lord Brougham said that "though called a cottage, because it happened to be thatched, it was still a very comfortable residence for a family". Here, in this rustic setting made picturesque with honeysuckle and peacocks, George IV spent his later and more unpopular years, shunning the public gaze and finding pleasure in the rare plants in his "Gothic" conservatory of cast iron, or driving in his curricle to his Chinese fishing temple at Virginia Water. Under the influence of Sir Jeffrey Wyatville all traces of this fanciful dwelling, "in a habit of unspoiled magnificence", were

[23]

swept away to be replaced by the house which was the favourite residence of George VI.

Balmoral Castle, the Queen's private residence in Scotland, owes its existence to the pleasure derived by Queen Victoria and Prince Albert from the peaceful life of the Highlands. When the Queen first saw it in 1848, she wrote, "It was so calm and so solitary. All seemed to breathe freedom and peace, and to make one forget the world and its sad turmoils". The estate, high above sea-level between Crathie and Braemar, was first leased and then purchased by the Prince Consort in 1852. Here he built a great granite castle, with a tower a hundred feet high. At his death in 1862 it was bequeathed to Queen Victoria, who delighted to live there. Her successors have used it as a summer residence.

Sandringham, a country house near the Norfolk coast, stands on an estate which was purchased by Edward VII, when Prince of Wales, from money saved during his minority. In 1871 the existing house was pulled down and replaced by an architecturally undistinguished mansion in red brick. This was the favourite home of George V, where the routine of life proceeded in many ways that lit up his sterling characteristics—the superb standard of its farming, its fine shooting, its clocks synchronized in their ticking and all kept exactly half an hour fast.

The most famous houses inhabited by members of the Royal Family other than the Monarch are Marlborough House, the residence of Queen Mary, and Clarence House, until recently the home of Princess Elizabeth and the Duke of Edinburgh and later to be occupied by Queen Elizabeth, the Queen Mother. Marlborough House was built for the first Duke of Marlborough on the site of an old pheasantry belonging to the Crown. No contrast could be sharper than that between this plain, dignified, brick mansion and

Vanbrugh's heroic palace of stone at Blenheim, with which a grateful nation honoured the great soldier a few years later. The house came into the possession of the Crown in 1810. It was inhabited by George IV's daughter, Princess Charlotte, and by Queen Adelaide during her widowhood. In 1863 it was altered and enlarged to become the residence of the Prince and Princess of Wales. For nearly forty years, and especially during the period of Queen Victoria's reluctance to take part in public life, it was socially as important as Buckingham Palace. Here were held the celebrated Derby Day dinners and those other functions by which the future Edward VII removed the throne from its former isolation and by his love of hospitality and pageantry placed himself at the head of his people, who shared his tastes to the full.

Clarence House has had a very different history. At the end of the eighteenth century the Duke of Clarence, the third son of George III, lived on this site in a strange jumble of rooms. After his marriage to Princess Adelaide he complained to his brother, George IV, of "the wretched state and dirt", so John Nash was employed to rebuild the house. When in 1830 the Duke of Clarence came to the throne as William IV, Buckingham Palace was still in the hands of the builders and the King disliked using St. James's Palace because he had to move his books every time a levée was held, so he continued to live in this very undistinguished house. In 1866, when Queen Victoria's second son, Prince Alfred, was made Duke of Edinburgh, Clarence House became his residence. He lived there for nearly thirty years and retained it as his London home after he became Duke of Saxe-Coburg and Gotha in 1893. Many improvements in the house were made to his own designs but something of its original inconvenience lasted through his tenancy and that of his brother, the Duke of Connaught. When the house was altered for Princess Elizabeth in 1947 it was found that it contained no bathrooms.

Of Hampton Court Palace and Kensington Palace, both used partly as museums and partly as apartments granted by favour of the Monarch, this is no place to give a detailed history. Both are buildings of great historic interest and both bear witness to the genius of Sir Christopher Wren. It was late in his career that he was commissioned by William III to rebuild Cardinal Wolsey's old house at Hampton Court and Nottingham House, Kensington—more than thirty years after John Evelyn had described him as "that miracle of a youth". Hampton Court was dilapidated when Wren started to work there. The beautiful Long Gallery was demolished but the equally beautiful Great Hall was preserved and remains today, an ineffably Elizabethan introduction to the Augustan elegance of Wren's State Apartments, overlooking the gardens, the Long Water, and the Thames. These garden buildings, constructed in thin, mulberry-coloured brick, with their correct accompaniments of wrought-iron screens and water vistas, are as beautiful as anything in England.

In only one small building did Wren exceed his own achievement; this was in the Orangery at Kensington, perhaps the last work of his extreme old age, built for Queen Anne as "her Summer Supper House". When William III bought Nottingham House in 1689, as a country residence within easy reach of London, he engaged Wren to make additions and alterations. Little of this work remains today and the palace as it stands is mostly from the designs of William Kent for Queen Caroline, the enlightened consort of George II. She did much to beautify the grounds of the palace, a charming occupation for which she had the inspiration of two of the most beautiful garden buildings

[26]

in England—Wren's Orangery and his alcove overlooking the fountains. The Queen gave a new distinction to the gardens by forming the Serpentine in 1733, even as she gave distinction to the house by hanging the wonderful drawings by Holbein of the Court of Henry VIII, which had just been found stored away in a cupboard. But there can be no doubt that the greatest event of this quiet, suburban palace occurred in the early morning of 20th June, 1837. Princess Victoria was awakened by her mother with the news that the Archbishop of Canterbury and the Lord Chamberlain were waiting to announce to her the death of her uncle and her own accession to the throne. The new Queen wrote in her journal, "Since it has pleased Providence to place me in this station, I shall do my utmost to fulfil my duty towards my country". The Queen recognized the affection in which the place of her birth and accession would always be held by her people and she opened the gardens to the public.

Palaces and castles no longer used by the Monarch make a long and distinguished list. The Tower of London, commenced in its present form by William I, was for centuries a royal residence. The heir to the throne was always lodged there for safety at the time of the death of the Sovereign. From the Tower started the State Procession on the day before the coronation, an essential element in the ancient elective ceremony which was preserved as late as the coronation of Charles II.

The great Palace of Whitehall was the permanent centre of the Court during the reigns of the Stuart monarchs. They made it larger than the Louvre, but, unlike the French palace, it was a chaotic jumble of buildings. One only of its buildings had claim to great distinction —the Banqueting House, built by Inigo Jones for James I

[27]

in 1622. This splendid edifice—it has been called "the most beautiful building in London"—was associated with two of the most formative events of the seventeenth century. It was from an upper window that Charles I stepped out to his execution in 1649, and in the great hall itself the English Crown was offered to the Prince and Princess of Orange in 1689. Only nine years later, through the carelessness of a Dutch laundress brought over by William and Mary, a fire caused the destruction of those twenty-three acres of closely-packed buildings—all, except the Banqueting House. As we look at it today we can well believe that the failure of the Stuart kings to carry out Inigo Jones's designs for a complete and homogeneous Palace of Whitehall is as much to be regretted as the City fathers' failure to allow Sir Christopher Wren to rebuild London after the Great Fire.

The beautiful Queen's House, with its airy and graceful interior, built by Inigo Jones for Henrietta Maria, still stands at Greenwich, now used as part of the National Maritime Museum. Frogmore, the home of Queen Charlotte, consort of George III, with the Royal Mausoleum erected by Queen Victoria, a richly adorned cruciform building, is within the Great Park at Windsor. Osborne, the seaside residence built by Queen Victoria and Prince Albert on the Isle of Wight, was one of the Queen's favourite homes. Here she died in 1901 and, just as she had commemorated her beloved husband by commanding that the Blue Room, at Windsor Castle, in which he died, should remain as he left it, so it was felt that, allowing for other times and other personalities, her son was honouring her in similar manner when he presented Osborne to the nation on his coronation day, 1902. By the King's desire part of the house was made a convalescent home for officers of the navy and army.

One of the most fantastic residences ever built by a monarch is still standing at Brighton. This is George IV's marine pavilion—not the one in Graeco-Roman style by Henry Holland but the Hindu "mosque" or "Kremlin" with which John Nash supplanted the earlier building in 1817. It is now the property of the municipality, having been sold by Queen Victoria when she built her seaside house at Osborne. Not only has the pavilion withstood the onslaughts of time and the mockery of its detractors but it has succeeded in keeping many of its original furnishings, so that those who are willing to be delighted by the architecture of pleasure may still wander through bamboo corridors, amongst gilt pagodas ten storeys high, under chandeliers in the shape of colossal dragons and gigantic water-lilies, pause where courtiers danced, and linger where a king made music.

Where royalty has lived there are always memories, even if the palaces themselves have vanished. There is a melancholy attraction in wandering for a moment amongst ruins that have known the stir of great events—to stand under the gateway, all that now remains of Richmond Palace, and recall that winter's day in 1603 when Queen Elizabeth, consumed with melancholy, turned her face to the wall and died; to walk under the flowering trees at Kew and remember the palace which George III bought in 1781 as a nursery for the royal children; to loiter where St. James's Street meets Pall Mall, trying to recapture from books and prints "that chaste palace" behind its Ionic screen—Carlton House, the epitome of Regency taste, built by Henry Holland in a style of rich simplicity, destined to last for but thirty years before it was swept away by its owner's restless passion for the latest fashion. There are many such ghosts of palaces—let these be their representatives.

3. Royal Occasions

I<small>T</small> was an ancient privilege of English gentlemen to have the right, without undue formality, to enter the presence of the Sovereign. Charles II, a monarch of engaging sociability, delighted in this custom. Pepys's record proves that he extended it even to mealtimes. "By and by the King to dinner, and I waited there his dining; but, Lord! how little I should be pleased, I think, to have so many people crowding about me." This was the origin of the Entrée—a privilege which has been severely restricted during the past two hundred and fifty years and is now granted only to Cabinet Ministers and their wives, to foreign Ambassadors, Ministers, and Chargés d'Affaires, to certain members of the Royal Household, and a few other distinguished persons. At Courts and other royal functions held at Buckingham Palace these guests are permitted to use a special door to the Palace, called the Ambassadors' Entrance. They are thus able to arrive after and leave before the general company and to pass the presence first, in what is called the Diplomatic Circle.

The main purpose of these Courts, Drawing Rooms and Levées is to enable Her Majesty's subjects to offer proof of their loyalty and respect for the institutions of Great Britain, through a carefully controlled system of presentation. Restriction of entrance has inevitably caused these events to become socially fashionable. It is in that light that they are now usually regarded and sometimes criticized but their place in the growth of popularity of the Monarch is not to be overlooked.

Queen Victoria severely curtailed Court ceremonies after the death of the Prince Consort, as part of a withdrawal from public life for which she incurred outspoken criticism in the newspapers. When she commenced to hold Courts again in 1864 a limited number of distinguished persons only was invited. But, as the years passed and as the enthusiasm greeting her appearances grew to heights never experienced by any other British monarch, the numbers permitted to attend were increased to as many as three thousand at each Drawing Room—so many, in fact, that the Queen believed the whole system might break down. In her old age it was a valuable link between the Queen and the vast number of her subjects and other nationals who had been personally introduced to her.

Presentations of ladies take place at Courts or Drawing Rooms, those of gentlemen at Levées, now in abeyance. A lady who has herself been presented may make application to the Lord Chamberlain to be summoned to attend at Court for the purpose of presenting one lady, for whom she must be responsible, in addition to her daughter or daughter-in-law. They may be accompanied to Court by their husbands if the latter have been presented. Commands to attend are not issued more than once in three years. Ladies of foreign nationality are only presented through the diplomatic representatives of their country.

The regulations governing His Majesty's Levées permitted any gentleman who had been presented to make application to attend, even if he did not wish to present his son or another gentleman. Those who had received the honour of knighthood were expected to be presented at the next Levée. It was customary, though not obligatory, for officers of the armed forces and the higher officials of the Civil Service to be presented on appointment and to attend on the occasion of their promotion. A levée is the only Court function from which ladies are excluded. In the latter part of the reign of Queen Victoria, her son, the Prince of Wales, frequently held Levées on Her Majesty's behalf.

Courts are held in the Ballroom at Buckingham Palace, the largest and most handsome of the State Apartments. When the Queen has taken her place on the throne dais at the west end of the room, the ceremony of presentation commences. The Marshal of the Diplomatic Corps leads the wife of the Secretary of State for Foreign Affairs to the dais. She makes her obeisance and then stands by the Queen while the ladies of the Diplomatic Corps pass the presence. Similarly, the Secretary of State for Foreign Affairs is conducted to the dais while the members of the Diplomatic Corps file past the Queen, each member being introduced by the Ambassador or Minister. The Secretary of State makes his bow and stands to one side while those who have the privilege of Entrée pass Her Majesty. These are followed by the General Circle, including the débutantes. Each name is announced to the Queen by the Lord Chamberlain. The correct form of obeisance for the débutantes is a deep curtsy. Before the war ladies attending a Court were required to wear low evening dresses with Court trains suspended from the shoulder. Veils with three small ostrich feathers mounted as a Prince of Wales plume were worn on the head.

Drawing Rooms are slightly less formal occasions than the Courts. They are now seldom held but were popular during the reign of Queen Victoria as a means of relieving the strain on a Monarch who disliked ceremony and who

The Round Tower, Windsor Castle

The Queen shakes hands with some of her guests during the first Garden Party of her reign held in the grounds of Buckingham Palace and attended by seven thousand people

The Throne Room, Buckingham Palace

found her health unequal to the task of making many public appearances in addition to her manifold State duties. These Drawing Rooms were usually held for the Queen by the Princess of Wales. Later in the reign they were held by the Queen herself, when her popularity caused so many ladies to attend that there were complaints in the newspapers of the hardships suffered by ladies of standing for six hours in a crowd without refreshment. The Queen permitted alterations to be made but did not approve of tea being provided, as it would turn a Drawing Room into a party.

The Royal Garden Parties in the beautiful grounds of Buckingham Palace are the most informal of all these Court functions. The Queen moves freely among her guests. Many introductions are made to her, but these do not normally count as equivalent to presentation at a Court or attendance at a Levée. An exception to this rule occurred in 1936, when Edward VIII held two Garden Parties of a more formal nature. They were Receptions, and presentations made to the King on those occasions were considered equivalent to presentation at Court.

Of the other State functions presided over by the Monarch none is more imposing than the State Banquets. These are held at Buckingham Palace or Windsor Castle when a foreign Sovereign or Chief of State pays an official visit to this country. On such an occasion the Royal gold plate is set out. The most remarkable pieces are the superb collection of Salts and the Wine Fountain made for Charles II by the Corporation of Plymouth. Of the Salts the earliest is Queen Elizabeth I's and the most magnificent is the Great Salt of State, made in the shape of a castle. This was a gift from the City of Exeter to Charles II on his restoration. The sweet course is served on the Garter china service. There is only one toast, that of the visitor, proposed by the Sovereign, to which the visitor replies. The Yeomen of the Guard are on duty on these occasions.

State Balls have always been functions of great magnificence. Commands to attend are amongst the most highly prized of privileges. At one time there was a belief that persons who had been presented at Court had a claim to be asked to a Ball. Queen Victoria expressed herself firmly on this question in 1874, when she said that invitations must always be given at the Queen's discretion and that no one socially or politically could lay the slightest claim to them.

In 1662 Samuel Pepys was a spectator at a State Ball at Whitehall and saw the King lead a lady in a single Coranto, "and then the rest of the Lords, one after another, other ladies: very noble it was, and great pleasure to see". The procedure described by Pepys was followed until 1924, the King and Queen opening the Ball with a Royal Quadrille. As George V dispensed with the Quadrilles at the Jubilee Celebration Balls in 1935, these were called Court Balls. In place of the opening dance by the King and Queen there is now a ceremonial procession when the Sovereign, preceded by the Lord Chamberlain, the Master of the Horse, and other officers of the Royal Household, enters the Ballroom and is conducted to a golden chair on a dais hung with crimson velvet.

On all occasions to which invitations by royal command are issued, the State Apartments are guarded by the personal escort of the Sovereign, the Queen's Bodyguard of the Honourable Corps of Gentlemen-at-Arms. This "nearest guard" was created by Henry VIII at his accession in 1509, when it was called the "Gentlemen Speres". The King, in rivalry of the French king's magnificent corps of *Pensionnaires*, changed the name to the Gentlemen Pensioners

[34]

in 1539. Until the seventeenth century the Corps retained its original composition of young noblemen of splendid personal appearance, whose families were of proved loyalty to the Sovereign. They were formed as a personal guard within the precincts of the Court. But with the rise of professional armies the Corps, clinging to its tradition of noble birth, became less and less military. The danger of this development was proved during the Chartist demonstration of 1848, when the Corps was summoned to guard St. James's Palace.

In 1862 the existing organization was created, by which only military officers who have received a war decoration are eligible for appointment. Their uniforms have always been gorgeous, especially in the reign of Elizabeth I, who had a high regard for her Gentlemen Pensioners. For his elaborate coronation George IV reconstructed the Tudor uniform from the famous picture of Queen Elizabeth on her way to Blackfriars. This archaic dress was not long in use, as the present uniform of scarlet swallow-tailed coat, blue overalls, and brass helmet with drooping white plume was introduced by William IV in 1834 at the same time that he granted the petition of the Corps to be known as the Honourable Corps of Gentlemen-at-Arms. A genuine survival of the early days of the Corps is the pole-axe still carried by the Gentlemen-at-Arms when on duty.

Duties similar to those of the Gentlemen-at-Arms are performed in Scotland by the Royal Company of Archers, the Queen's Bodyguard for Scotland. The earliest records of this Company date from 1676, but tradition links these noblemen and gentlemen, associating for the encouragement of archery, with the archer guard of the kings of Scotland. Queen Anne granted a charter to the Royal Company by which they had access to all archery fields in return for a reddendo consisting of one pair of barbed arrows. Only eleven reddendos have so far been claimed, the latest being by Queen Elizabeth II at Holyroodhouse in June 1952. On this occasion the reddendo took the form of a brooch with three crossed golden arrows, flecked with diamonds. It is curious that though the charter specifies a pair of arrows, it is always a group of three arrows that is presented.

The ceremony of the reddendo is one of the most picturesque in the whole range of British pageantry. The Royal Company, two hundred and fifty strong, is drawn up in two ranks. They wear their field uniforms, consisting of dark green tunics, trousers trimmed with black and crimson, Balmoral bonnets with the thistle badge and tall eagle's feathers. They hold upright their long yew bows while the reddendo is offered to the Sovereign on a green velvet cushion.

As no Sovereign had visited Scotland for one hundred and seventy years the visit of George IV in 1822 was an event of some significance. He marked the occasion by appointing the Royal Company to be the King's Bodyguard for Scotland and constituted the Company as part of the Royal Household by presenting to the Captain-General a gold stick. His successor, William IV, placed this great honour on a permanent basis by making the senior officers Gold and Silver Sticks for Scotland, thus permitting them to share with the Lord High Constable of Scotland the same supreme responsibilities for the safety of the Monarch which rest upon Gold and Silver Sticks in England. At the same time the seven members of the Council, the governing body of the Royal Archers, were permitted to carry ebony sticks. George IV, with his passion for splendid clothes, added to the field dress and Court dress already worn by the Archers, an elaborate full-dress uniform.

4. *Household Troops*

THE oldest Household corps in England is the Queen's Bodyguard of the Yeoman of the Guard. Founded in 1485 by Henry VII after the Battle of Bosworth, before which time no English King "used such a furniture of daily soldiers", in Hall's words, the guard has had a continuous and distinguished history.

In the early days the Yeomen were the King's personal attendants day and night, at home and abroad. Six hundred of them protected Henry VIII when he went to visit Francis I of France on the Field of the Cloth of Gold. Since the Guy Fawkes plot in 1605 they have searched the vaults of the Houses of Parliament at the opening of each session. In 1743 they were present at the Battle of Dettingen as George II's personal attendants. A relic of one of their most important functions still exists in the letters Y.B.H. (Yeoman Bed-Hangers) and Y.B.G. (Yeoman Bed-Goers) which appear after the names of some of the Yeomen. In the days of the Tudor Monarchs these guards were the only persons permitted to make and examine the King's bed. Their commanding officer is called the Captain and the junior officers are given the curious title of Exons. The uniform of the Yeoman, now one of the most picturesque of any armed force in the world, has been altered many times but was brought back to something near its Tudor original by George IV. It was Edward VII, himself bearded, who introduced the practice of the Yeoman wearing beards, thus heightening the Elizabethan appearance. Wearing their scarlet doublets, embroidered with the emblems of the three kingdoms, and black velvet Tudor hats and bearing their long partizans, they are a welcome feature of many State occasions—guarding the royal coach to and from Parliament, at the distribution of Maundy Money on Holy Thursday, and on duty near the Royal Box during State visits to the Royal Opera House. Officers, since the time of William IV, are dressed in the uniform of a field officer of the Peninsular period. It is possible that they are nicknamed "Beefeaters" from the comment of the Grand Duke Cosimo of Tuscany in 1669 that "they are great eaters of beef, of which a very large ration is given them daily at the court". There is sometimes confusion between the Yeomen and the Warders of the Tower, owing to the similarity of their dress. The Warders are not Yeomen of the Guard, perform no State functions and are controlled by the Constable of the Tower. Edward VI granted permission to them to wear the uniform, as a mark of special favour.

Of all regiments of the British Army those most brilliantly associated with ceremonial are the three regiments of Household Cavalry. Consisting of two regiments of Life Guards and one regiment of Royal Horse Guards (The Blues), they occupy a position in which they combine the ceremonial functions of a royal escort with the military duties of mounted and now mechanized detachments. Their position close to the Monarch is emphasized by the appointment of the two Colonels to share, month by month, the high office of Gold Stick-in-Waiting. The Lieutenant-Colonel commanding the Household Cavalry, who may be of any of the regiments, shares the office of Silver Stick with officers of the Gentlemen-at-Arms. The Life Guards were founded for the personal protection of the Monarch in 1659, during

Charles II's exile. The Blues, although of equal antiquity, were not raised to the status of Household Cavalry until 1820, when they were granted the honour in recognition of their great achievements at Waterloo.

The daily duty of these regiments is to find the Queen's Life Guard at Whitehall. The Guard, riding with almost straight legs on their black horses, not rising in the saddle, is one of the most splendid sights in London. They wear plumed steel helmets, cuirasses, and thigh boots, stiffly "jacked" with wax, the Life Guards being in scarlet tunics, the Horse Guards in blue. The squadron standard is carried by a Corporal-Major, the equivalent of a sergeant-major in other regiments. As the Guard passes Buckingham Palace on its way from the Hyde Park barracks, the mounted trumpeter sounds a short salute. The changing of the Guard takes place at eleven in the morning at the Horse Guards, where there has been a guard every day since 1751, except for two years during the Second World War. The uniforms of the three regiments, which may be studied in detail by those who pass the two boxmen in Whitehall, have a number of minute peculiarities. The plumes vary from spun whalebone, to horsehair and yak's hair, the flash cords are red and blue, the shabracques are blue with rounded tips and red with pointed tips, the saddles are covered with white goatskin and black lambskin. Another mark of their connexion with the Royal Household is that the officers wear aiguillettes hung from the right shoulder, as do Equerries and officers of the Corps of Gentlemen-at-Arms and the Yeomen of the Guard, non-commissioned officers wearing them, as do the royal footmen, from the left shoulder.

The Household Cavalry have the duty of providing escorts on all State occasions. The most spectacular of these is the Sovereign's Escort, when one hundred and sixteen

Guardsmen ride with drawn swords, the Corporal-Major has the distinction of bearing the Royal Standard, and the Farrier Corporals of Horse wear their special blue uniform, with a black plume, and carry a large and highly polished axe, shaped like a tomahawk. The seven officers of this escort have gold cross belts, cuirass belts, and sword slings; the chargers of the Life Guards have gold reins and their hooves are specially polished. A Captain's Escort with Standard is used to escort the Sovereign to a Levée at St. James's Palace, while a Captain's Escort without Standard accompanies other members of the Royal Family and royal guests. The heir to the throne has a special escort under a subaltern. A Travelling Escort is used when the Sovereign does not wear full dress.

The bands of the Household Cavalry are famous for their State uniform of heavily gold-laced frock-coats, black velvet jockey caps, and long white gaiters. This is worn on ceremonial occasions only and is the same for the Life Guards and the Blues. At other times they wear regimental uniform. Originally these bands consisted of trumpeters and kettle-drummers only, negro musicians being often employed in the hundred years between George II and Queen Victoria. The trumpeters in their State uniform attend many functions independent of the band. The drummers ride the famous skewbald stallions from Holland. When playing mounted the musicians control the horses by reins attached to the stirrup irons.

The five regiments of Foot Guards, known as the Brigade of Guards, consist of the Grenadier Guards, the Coldstream Guards, the Scots Guards, the Irish Guards and the Welsh Guards. The first two have rival claims to seniority, the Grenadiers being descended from a regiment that served with Charles II in exile, the Coldstreamers from the Lord

The Queen and the Duke of Edinburgh driving up the course on the opening day of the Royal Meeting at Ascot, June 1952

The Colour being trooped by the Third Battalion Grenadier Guards before the Queen (then Princess Elizabeth) on the Sovereign's Birthday Parade

General's Foot Guards, a crack regiment of the New Model army of the Commonwealth. The Scots Guards were brought on to the English Establishment at the time of the Act of Union in 1707 but had existed as the Scots Foot Guards in the seventeenth century. There was a regiment of Irish Guards in Charles II's army but it was disbanded in 1698 and the present regiment was raised by the express wish of Queen Victoria in recognition of the services rendered by Irish regiments in the South African War. The Welsh Guards, the youngest of these great regiments, was raised in 1915, and the equality of honour thus established between all the countries of the Union was recognized in 1950 when the motto of the Brigade was changed to *Quinque Juncta in Uno*.

The uniforms of the regiments are similar in that they all wear scarlet tunics, with blue collars, cuffs and shoulder straps, blue trousers and high bearskin caps. The differences are most noticeable in the badges, the grouping of the buttons and the colour of the plumes. The Grenadiers have a flaming grenade, buttons evenly spaced and a plume of white goat's hair (the shaving brush); the Coldstreams, a Garter star, buttons in pairs and a red plume; the Scots Guards, a thistle, buttons in threes and no plume; the Irish Guards, a shamrock, buttons in fours and a plume of blue cut feathers; the Welsh Guards, a leek, buttons in two groups of five and a longer plume of white cut feathers.

Of all the companies of the Brigade of Guards none is more distinguished than the Queen's Company of the Grenadier Guards. George VI said of them that they are "on the right of the line of British infantry". On guard-mounting duty they carry a special Queen's Colour presented by the Sovereign herself, the old one being buried with the late sovereign. Until the death of Edward VII it was the

[41]

prerogative of the Household Cavalry to undertake all military duties inside the Royal palaces, but the King's Company were then granted the privilege of guarding the King's body between the time of death and the public lying-in-state. They are on duty at Westminster Abbey at the coronation. In the Welsh Guards there is a Prince of Wales's Company.

The regiments of the Brigade of Guards are familiar to everyone in London from their guard duties at the Royal palaces. The Queen's Guard consists of two detachments, one at Buckingham Palace, the other at St. James's Palace. When the Court is absent from London each detachment is reduced in size and the Changing of the Guard takes place on the Colour Court at St. James's Palace. But when the Queen is in London the guard-mounting ceremony, with the full guard, is seen to advantage in the spacious setting of the forecourt of Buckingham Palace. The new guard comes on duty to the music of the drums and fifes, the Ensign, equivalent to a second-lieutenant in other regiments, bearing the Colour. When the two guards are assembled in the forecourt they commence a stately ritual that is the delight of the watching crowd. The climax of the drill is the passing of the new guard in slow time before the old guard, the Colour being dipped for twenty paces. As the whole detachment moves at right angles to the Palace the band plays the regimental march—if it is the Grenadiers, the March from *Scipio*, which Handel wrote specially for them. The sentries are posted, the lieutenants hand over the Guard Room at St. James's Palace, the Captains exchange the keys, and the old guard marches away with its drums and fifes.

The headquarters of the Queen's Guard is in the maze of courts and buildings that make up St. James's Palace. Here is the officers' mess built in 1793, in which a good table is maintained every night through the munificence of George IV. The officer of the Queen's Life Guard at Whitehall has the right to dine here with the officers of the Queen's Guard. For this ceremonial visit he wears regimental mess kit, helmet and cloak, and carries a slung sword. He is due back at the Horse Guards by 11 p.m. and must give the pass-word. On the other side of the alley from the officers' mess is the guard dining-hall, originally the great kitchen of St. James's Palace, built by Vanbrugh for the Prince of Wales in 1716.

There are two other ancient duties performed by the Brigade of Guards, which, though they take place every day, are not often seen by the public. These are the Ceremony of the Keys at the Tower of London and the Guard Mounting at the Bank of England. The former is well known through frequent broadcasts. The routine of locking up this great royal fortress, treasure-house, and prison, has remained unchanged for centuries—the Chief Warder, with his lantern and keys, locking the gates of the towers, the challenge by the sentry of the Brigade of Guards at the Bloody Tower, "Halt! who goes there?" "The Keys." "Whose keys?" "Queen Elizabeth's keys." "Pass Queen Elizabeth's keys, all's well"; the salute to the keys by the main guard as they present arms; the Chief Warder doffing his hat and crying "God preserve Queen Elizabeth", to which the guard and escort reply "Amen", and then, as the clock strikes ten, the sounding of the Last Post by the drummer and the locking of the Tower for the night.

The long march of the Bank Picquet from Wellington Barracks to the City is less known. Many people on their way home from work in the gloom of a winter evening, must have seen and wondered as the twenty guardsmen,

[43]

with their officer and three non-commissioned officers, passed through the City, not realizing that these men and their predecessors have been doing this night duty for over a hundred and seventy years. In 1780 the Brigade of Guards was called out at a time of dire emergency, to protect the Bank from the fury of the anti-Catholic mob led by Lord George Gordon. The rioting lasted for days; at one time it seemed that Westminster and the City were at the mercy of Gordon and his hooligans. It was only with the loss of many hundreds of lives that order was restored. From this bloodthirsty episode has sprung the custom of the night guard at the Bank.

The bands of the Guards regiments are amongst the finest in the British Army. On royal occasions and anniversaries the Drum Majors wear State dress, similar to the beautiful gold-embroidered Stuart dresses of the trumpeters of the Household Cavalry. There are other customs peculiar to these bands—they never use bugles on parade, side drums being used instead; no flourishes of drum sticks or staves are permitted; the "time beaters" of the Grenadiers wear a dark band on their arms. The drums, fifes, and pipes are not part of the bands but are used for operational purposes only.

The most splendid ceremony in which the Brigade takes part—the Household Cavalry and all five regiments of Foot Guards—is the Queen's Birthday Parade, often incorrectly called Trooping the Colour. This, the finest military display of our time, is held on the Sovereign's official birthday.

It is a highly complex ceremonial consisting of four parts, the inspection of the troops by the Queen, the Trooping the Colour itself, which is a part of the old ceremony of mounting a guard on a person of royal blood, the march past, and the procession back to Buckingham Palace. The cere-

mony takes place on the Horse Guards Parade in front of
the quietly distinguished building designed by William
Kent two hundred years ago as the headquarters of the army.
The parade ground, the largest ceremonial open space in
London, was originally the Tiltyard built by Henry VIII
for jousting. The gallery from which Queen Elizabeth I
watched the tournaments was called the Fortress of Perfect
Beauty. At eleven o'clock on a summer morning the
Queen, surrounded by the glittering escort of the Household
Cavalry, rides slowly across the ground to the saluting point
in front of the Horse Guards Arch and salutes the Colour.
Facing her, across the great width from the Foreign Office
to the Admiralty, is the long line of the Foot Guards. After
the formal inspection, to the sound of drum-taps and words
of command, the Trooping begins, with the magnificent
slow movement of the massed bands across the front of the
line, repeated immediately, as are all the movements in this
ritual, in quick time. The Colour is solemnly handed to
the Ensign and, with the Escort for the Colour, he takes it
very slowly past the motionless ranks of Guards, "trooping"
it in accordance with the tradition of reminding the soldiers
of their duty to God and Sovereign of which the Colour is
the symbol. Then, in slow time and in quick time, the
Foot Guards and the Household Cavalry march past in
column. The Brigade mounts a Queen's Guard and with
their beloved Sovereign at their head they march off the
Horse Guards Parade—the Queen in scarlet and blue, riding
side-saddle, the flash of steel and the nodding of red and
white plumes from the Household Cavalry, the sumptuous
gold surcoats and black Montero caps of the State trumpeters
and drummers, the steadily moving lines of scarlet men—
swinging into the Mall and so back to Buckingham Palace.

This stately act of allegiance to the throne, and the Queen's status as Colonel-in-Chief of the five regiments of Foot Guards, serve as reminders of those other symbols of the ancient martial pre-eminence of the Sovereign—the royal arms and the royal standard. The science of heraldry, introduced into England from the Continent in the twelfth century, was concerned with establishing and maintaining in perfect form the devices by which kings and great noblemen displayed their lineage, their dignity, or their office.

The royal arms is specially distinguished in heraldry, in that it is composed of the charges of the countries over which the monarch claims to rule. Thus until 1801 the Fleurs de Lys of France appeared on the royal shield of Great Britain. William III charged his paternal shield of Nassau and George I introduced the arms of Hanover. Today the four quarters of the royal shield contain the three lions passant guardant of England in the first and fourth quarters, the lion of Scotland within a double frame called a tressure in the second, and the harp of Ireland in the third. The supporters are a lion rampant guardant and a unicorn rampant, English and Scottish devices which came together at the time of the Act of Union of 1707. It is from that time that the traditional rivalry of the lion and the unicorn is said to date. Before the Union a dragon or a greyhound supported the English royal shield with the lion. The Scottish kings used two silver unicorns. There is a theory that these heraldic beasts may have found their way into the royal heraldry of the United Kingdom from the French ceremonial of testing the royal food for poison with a unicorn's horn. The royal crest is a golden lion statant guardant, standing on an Imperial crown. The lion crest was first assumed by Edward III and has been retained ever since, with the Imperial crown added. The royal motto is the ancient Norman war-cry *Dieu et Mon Droit* ("God and my Right"). This was first used regularly by Henry VI and has been used by all monarchs since, although Queen Elizabeth and Queen Anne also used *Semper Eadem* ("Always the Same") and James I also used *Beati Pacifici* ("Blessed are the Peace-makers").

In 1883 an Act was passed preventing the unauthorized use of the royal arms but this regulation is still often unintentionally broken by patriotic people who use the royal standard on days of celebration. The design of the standard is the royal coat of arms, so that it is the Sovereign's personal banner. Its use is a mark of the actual presence of the Queen, with the exception that Edward VII granted to Westminster Abbey the privilege of flying the standard when the Sovereign is in its neighbourhood—for instance, during the State Opening of Parliament. Until 1828 the Lord High Admiral had the right to fly the standard when in executive command of a fleet. Its design has altered as often as the devices of the royal arms were changed by different kings.

From the days of Henry VIII it has been a constitutional principle that on the death of a sovereign his heir immediately becomes the successor to the throne, and therefore, since the Crown never dies, the royal standard is never flown at half-mast as a sign of mourning. "The King is dead. Long Live the King!"

5. The Royal Household

THE Royal Household was originally the centre of the general system of government. The leading dignitaries of the Palace, the Sovereign's closest advisers, were, by the nature of a form of rule directly exercised by the King, also the principal administrators. This grouping of the operation of power can be traced to the Teutonic chieftains, who had three principal and powerful servants. The system was developed in Saxon England and, even more, in France and Normandy, where the heads of the three departments were the seneschal or steward, the chamberlain, and the constable. This arrangement of the ducal household of Normandy was copied in England after the Conquest. It was in keeping with the feudal spirit that these great offices should be made hereditary and so their holders gradually ceased to have direct control over the conduct of affairs. They appeared on occasions of great ceremonial but their duties in the royal palace and many of their political functions were taken over by a second rank of officials who have become the effective heads of the three branches into which the Royal Household is still divided.

The earliest record of any of these officers is to be found in *The Black Book of the Exchequer*, prepared in the reign of Henry II. More information was added in *The Black Book of the Household*, written in the time of Edward IV but describing the Court as it was in the days of Edward III, who, it says, was "the first setter of certeynties among his

The Household Cavalry taking part in the Royal Windsor Horse Show in Windsor Home Park

The Ceremony of the Keys at the Tower of London

J. Stephanoff's drawing of Lord Charles Bentinck, Treasurer of the Household at the time of the coronation of George IV

J. Stephanoff's drawing of Sir Benjamin Bloomfield, Keeper of the Privy Purse at the time of the coronation of George IV

domesticall meyne, upon a grounded rule", and whose palace is described as "the house of very policie and flowre of England". But the records have always been meagre, and at the accession of Queen Victoria it was declared that Chamberlayne's *Present State of England* was the only authority for determining the appropriate constitution and dimension of the domestic establishment of a queen regnant. Even this was far from containing those certainties which were claimed to have been set down by Edward III, as Prince Albert found when he attempted to rationalize the confused state of affairs in the royal palaces.

The main divisions of the Royal Household are now substantially the same as they were in Plantagenet or Tudor times. The three departments, sometimes designated "below stairs", "above stairs", and "out of doors", are controlled by the Lord Steward, the Lord Chamberlain, and the Master of the Horse, respectively. The first dignitary of the Court is the Lord Steward. He ranks nineteenth in the order of precedence of the United Kingdom, but it is important to remember that there is no complete code of precedency in this country. He was at one time a member of the government and until 1782 always a Cabinet Minister. Today, he and the Lord Chamberlain are not necessarily members of the current administration but it yet remains that their names are always submitted to the Sovereign by the Prime Minister. From the Sovereign the Lord Steward receives his appointment in person and bears a white staff as emblem and warrant of his authority. His principal duty is to preside at the Board of Green Cloth, a committee of the Queen's Household charged with the examination and passing of all the accounts of the Household. The name of the committee is derived from the green-covered table at which its transactions were originally conducted. In his department

D

are the Treasurer and the Comptroller of the Household. Both of these, who are White Staff officers, are political appointments, changing with the ministry, and their duties are carried out by the Master of the Household.

This office is of more recent date than many of those in the Royal Household and is an example of the reforming zeal of Prince Albert. In 1844 he determined to bring order into the chaos of the Queen's establishment. He found that much of the confusion and discomfort was caused by the lack of co-ordination between the Lord Chamberlain, who was responsible for all rooms at Buckingham Palace (except the kitchens, sculleries, and pantries), the Lord Steward, who controlled these "below stairs" offices, and the Office of Woods and Forests, which had the oversight of the outside of the building. Each authority was independent and jealous of its venerable rights. The Office of Woods and Forests, particularly, caused the Queen exasperation. In 1837 she looked forward to having a home of her own, which would be "free from the Woods and Forests and other charming departments, which are really the plague of one's life". The Prince might never have succeeded in his laborious task if public attention had not been drawn to the abuses by the affair of "the boy Jones", who was able to remain undetected for three days in the Palace, helping himself to food and even sitting on the throne. In the end the Prince was completely successful and the conflicting authorities were induced to resign their powers to the Master of the Household, who was made responsible for the entire management of the royal palaces. He is a permanent official, resides at Buckingham Palace, is a White Staff officer and a member of the Board of Green Cloth. His domestic pre-eminence is signified by his presiding at the daily dinners of the suite in waiting on the Sovereign.

The Board of Green Cloth once had powers of jurisdiction and could punish offenders within the verge of the Palace. In addition, the Lord Steward presided over three courts, of which the earliest was superseded in 1541 by the Marshalsea Court. This had criminal and civil jurisdiction within an area of twelve miles from where the Sovereign was resident, and administered justice between the royal domestic servants. The third court, created in 1612, was the Palace Court, which had jurisdiction over all personal matters arising between parties within twelve miles of Whitehall but had no authority over the Sovereign's household. Both these courts were abolished in 1849, but a relic of the Marshalsea Court still exists in the Queen's Marshalmen who take their place at the coronation and one of whom is always on duty at the changing of the guard. Originally they were a form of Palace police, under the orders of the Lord Steward. With the abolition of the court their duties have become ceremonial, as is their dress with its scarlet coatee and blue doeskin trousers. They have now been transferred to the Lord Chamberlain's department. The Lord Steward or his deputies formerly administered the oath to members of the House of Commons, a duty now performed by the Speaker. But the Lord Steward's position as intermediary between the Sovereign and Parliament is still maintained by the fact that messages under the royal sign manual are conveyed to the Houses of Parliament by the lords with white staves.

The Lord Chamberlain is the second dignitary of the Court, ranking twentieth in the order of precedence of the United Kingdom. Before 1782 the office carried with it Cabinet rank. He has a white staff as a token of his authority and he wears a golden key as a symbol of his care of the royal palaces. From the scope and variety of his duties he may be regarded as the chief officer of the Royal Household. He is responsible for the arrangement of State ceremonies, such as coronations, royal weddings, christenings, and funerals. He examines the claims of all those who wish to be presented at Court—although there was at least one occasion on which Queen Victoria was better informed than her Lord Chamberlain and insisted on cancelling a presentation after it had been made. All invitations to State functions are sent out in his name by command of the Sovereign. At Courts and Levées he announces the names of persons approaching the throne. It is his privilege to conduct the Queen to and from her carriage.

The Lord Chamberlain's political deputy is the Vice-Chamberlain of the Household but the great range of duties within this department necessitates for its control a staff of expert permanent officials. There is the Ecclesiastical Household, containing the College of Chaplains and the Chaplains, Precentors, and Organists of the Chapels Royal. The head of the College is the Clerk of the Closet. He is usually a bishop and his duties were described a century ago as "to attend at the Right hand of the Sovereign in the Royal Closet during Divine Service, to resolve such doubts as may arise concerning spiritual matters". There are twenty-four chaplains to the Queen in England and nine in Scotland. In addition to these are the Dean and other ecclesiastical officials of the Chapels Royal at St. James's Palace and Hampton Court. The Chapel in the Savoy, off the Strand, was made a Chapel Royal in 1773. It had the privilege of being one of the last buildings in which it was possible for fugitives from justice to claim sanctuary. It is not under the jurisdiction of the Dean but is reserved to the visitation and immediate government of the Sovereign, thence deriving the name of "a Royal Peculiar".

Ranking high amongst the functionaries of the Court,

under the Lord Chamberlain, is the Gentleman Usher of the Black Rod, the principal usher of the Court and the kingdom, whose ensign of office is an ebony stick surmounted with a gold lion. His office came into existence with the foundation of the Order of the Garter in 1349 and he is still the usher of the Order. It is a proof of the age-old connexion between the Sovereign and Parliament that Black Rod is in constant attendance upon the House of Lords. Wearing his chain and badge of office and carrying the Black Rod, he bears all messages from the House of Lords to the House of Commons. Since 1642, when Charles I attempted to arrest five members of the House, the door is always shut in the face of Black Rod and he knocks three times and announces his office before he is admitted.

There are six Lords-in-Waiting and six Grooms-in-Waiting who attend on the Sovereign throughout the year, in periods of duty usually lasting two or three weeks at a time. The Serjeants-at-Arms are the most ancient guards waiting upon the Sovereign. They were first instituted by Richard I. Two of them form another royal link with Parliament, as they have the duty of attending the Speaker in the House of Commons and the Lord Chancellor in the House of Lords. They are appointed by Patent under the Great Seal and are charged with the maintenance of order in the Houses of Parliament. On State occasions the Serjeants-at-Arms bearing their great silver-gilt maces are seen walking before the Sovereign.

Through the Marshal of the Diplomatic Corps the Lord Chamberlain's Office controls the complicated ceremonial involved in the reception of foreign potentates and ambassadors. When a new *Chef de Mission* arrives in London one of his first duties is to present his credentials to the Sovereign. The Marshal calls on him and escorts him to the Palace in a

State landau. These are occasions of great formality and etiquette. Few of them can have been more open to possibilities of embarrassment than the ceremony in 1785 when John Adams, the first American ambassador, was received by George III, the king who had done everything to prevent the secession of the American colonies. Adams greeted him with the forthright statement, "I must avow to your Majesty that I have no attachment but to my own country."

The Lord Chamberlain has charge of the appointment of the royal physicians and surgeons, the royal librarian, the surveyors of the Queen's pictures and works of art, the keeper of the Jewel House, and the Royal Warrant holders, tradesmen who have the privilege of supplying goods to the Court. The latter may use the royal arms for trade purposes but may not fly the royal standard. False claims are punishable by law. The distinction is highly prized and is now more strictly limited than it was in other reigns, when there were warrants issued for a maker of waterproof dress clogs, a manufacturer of solid headed pins and a purveyor of *eau-de-bouquet*.

Two of the most picturesque of the ancient offices under the control of the Lord Chamberlain are those of the Queen's Bargemaster and the Keeper of the Swans. In the days when the Thames was the High Street of London the Bargemaster and his crew of thirty-four royal watermen were busily employed in transporting members of the Royal Family. Charles II had a yacht, presented to him by the Dutch East India Company, and a rich gondola sent as a gift by the Signory of Venice, as well as the great State barge, with its Corinthian pillars and its gilded cupola. In 1732 William Kent designed a magnificent Palladian barge for Frederick, Prince of Wales. This was afterwards used by George II and other monarchs until 1849, when it appeared for the last time to convey Queen Victoria and Prince Albert to the City for the opening of the new Coal Exchange. Today it is in the Victoria and Albert Museum, still showing in its white and gold elegance something of the delight of being rowed by the scarlet-coated royal watermen, to the strains of Handel's *Water Music*.

Some of the most interesting connexions of the Lord Chamberlain are with the arts. These are maintained in three directions—by the appointments of a Poet Laureate and a Master of the Queen's Music, and by the control of certain theatres and the texts of all plays when they are produced. The office of Poet Laureate, that is the poet attached to the Royal Household, was created by James I for Ben Jonson in 1617. Poets of earlier days, such as Chaucer and Spenser, had received royal patronage, Chaucer being the first to be granted the perquisite of wine which became a feature of the emoluments of the office. For many years the Laureate has drawn an allowance of £27 in lieu of "a butt of sack". The formal nature of the appointment was recognized in 1670, when Dryden received the title by Letters Patent. As a Court official, the Laureate produced appropriate verses on State occasions, but with the decay of the art of formal versifying this practice fell into disrepute. Wordsworth made it a condition of accepting the honour that no State poetry should be required of him. Tennyson, who succeeded him, found, on the other hand, attractions in ceremonial verse and produced several admirable examples of the State Ode. The present distinguished holder of the post is John Masefield.

The Master of the Queen's Music was originally the conductor of the Royal Band of Music, a company of musicians of which there are records as early as the reign of Edward IV. The composition of the band varied under different monarchs, around the essential elements of trumpets, drums, and

stringed and woodwind instruments. Edward VI had a
Welsh minstrel, Elizabeth a bagpiper, while Charles I added
hautboys and recorders, under the direction of Nicholas
Lanier, Master of the Band. At the Restoration, Charles II
established the famous stringed band popularly known as
"the four and twenty fiddlers", which played while the
King was at meals. In the eighteenth century the band was
employed in the performance of the odes composed by the
Poet Laureate every year for the King's birthday. With
the discontinuance of these performances the company of
royal musicians declined into a small wind-band, until Prince
Albert, whose informed enthusiasm for music has not always
been appreciated, reorganized the Queen's private band into
a full orchestra. State concerts were given which were a
feature of the social and musical life of London a hundred
years ago. Edward VII discontinued the concerts, and the
office of the Master of the Music, as it was held by Sir Edward
Elgar and now by Sir Arnold Bax, is of an advisory nature.

The Lord Chamberlain's connexion with the theatre relates
both to buildings and to plays. The regulations governing
the establishment of theatres stem from the privileges or
patents granted to certain royal theatres in London by
Charles II in 1662, when the theatrical profession was starting
again after the Commonwealth with virtually no places in
which to perform. In spite of the prohibition on non-
privileged buildings other playhouses gradually arose.

In 1737, Parliament, from motives of political control,
passed an Act which closely regulated the theatre for more
than a century. It made illegal the establishment of theatres
anywhere except in the City of Westminster and in places
where the King should in person reside, and then only during
his residence. Even the apparent relaxation in the case of
Westminster proved illusory, as in practice the Act was

operated to prevent performances of legitimate drama anywhere except at Drury Lane and Covent Garden, the two major patent houses, and the Theatre Royal in the Haymarket, which had a patent for the summer months only. During the lifetime of this Act Theatres Royal were established at Bath, Liverpool, Bristol, and other cities, but most of the provincial centres were deliberately starved. The passing of the Theatres Act in 1843 inaugurated a more liberal policy and its provisions are substantially in operation today. The Lord Chamberlain licenses all theatres in the metropolis, except the patent houses which are exempt from this control, the theatres in Windsor and Brighton, and theatres in places where the Sovereign occasionally resides, but only during the time of such residence. In the provinces buildings are licensed by the local authority, except at Oxford and Cambridge, where a licence by the local justices must receive the consent of the Chancellor or Vice-Chancellor of the University.

The censorship of plays, the second of the Lord Chamberlain's functions in relation to the theatre, derives from the office of the Master of the Revels, who in Elizabethan times kept a strong control over the details of performances, on behalf of his mistress. In 1624 these duties were transferred to his official superior, the Lord Chamberlain, in whose care they have been ever since. His powers were confirmed and regulated by the Acts of 1737 and 1843, so that every stage play must be licensed before performance. For this purpose a copy of the play must be lodged with a special officer in the Lord Chamberlain's department, known as the Examiner of Stage Plays. The powers of the censorship are seldom used for political reasons but are still invoked for the violation of the sentiments of religious reverence and for the representation in an invidious manner of a living person or a person recently dead. This has led to the temporary banning of *King Lear* during the insanity of George III and of *The Mikado* when its performance was thought likely to give offence to a Japanese prince.

When there is a Queen Consort, Her Majesty's Household is also in the department of the Lord Chamberlain. It consists of a Lord Chamberlain, a Treasurer, and the various ladies of the Royal Household, at the head of whom is the Mistress of the Robes. But under a Queen Regnant there is no need of a separate Household and then the Mistress of the Robes becomes one of the most important royal officials, superseding the Groom of the Robes and the more ancient office of the Groom of the Stole. The holder of this merged office has the duty of supervising the King's State garments. The Mistress of the Robes is the only lady of the Court whose appointment is recommended to the Sovereign by the Prime Minister. The changing of other ladies of the Household for political considerations ceased after the "bedchamber question" in 1839, when Queen Victoria expressed her disapproval of Sir Robert Peel's desire to remove some of the ladies against Her Majesty's wish. It was at Queen Victoria's accession that the precedent of the Lord Chamberlain's responsibility for obtaining the coronation robes was discarded and the arrangements for ordering what were called "Particulars", from the dalmatic of gold and silk brocade to the purple velvet shoes embroidered with rosebuds and "All hail Victoria" worked inside in gold thread, were placed in the hands of the Mistress of the Robes. The holder of the office was the Duchess of Sutherland, whom Queen Victoria thought "so handsome".

The third dignitary of the Court is the Master of the Horse. He is always a member of the administration, a peer, and a privy councillor. Before 1782 he was a Cabinet

Minister. He is officially responsible for all matters relating to the royal horses, hounds, stables, coachhouses, studs, mews, and kennels. In ceremonial duties he rides next behind the Sovereign in State processions. When there is a Queen Regnant he rides in the carriage with Her Majesty. The practical management of this "out of doors" department is in the hands of the Chief or Crown Equerry, who in former days was called the Gentleman of the Horse. The accounts are managed by the Clerk Marshal before they go to the Board of Green Cloth for payment. As the Lord Chamberlain is in charge of the Lords-in-Waiting who attend on the Sovereign at Court, so the Master of the Horse is responsible for the Equerries who accompany the Sovereign's carriage on all State occasions. Also in his department are the Pages of Honour, who should not be confused with Pages of the Backstairs, Pages of the Presence, and other royal servants controlled by the Lord Chamberlain. These Pages of Honour are younger members of titled families who are in attendance on the Sovereign at Courts and other State occasions. They are best known for their appearance at the coronation when, in their scarlet frocks decorated with gold lace, they assist the Groom of the Robes to carry the royal train.

It has been seen how the reforms of Prince Albert resulted in the creation of a new office, the Master of the Household, while preserving the traditional distinctions of the ancient Household offices. Two other changes of this nature occurred during the reign of George III, when the failing health of the Monarch was responsible for the appointment of a Private Secretary and a Keeper of the Privy Purse. These are personal officers of the Sovereign, having little connexion with the ceremonial of the Court. It is in the nature of their offices that they should be well known by name only but it is reasonable to assume that, with the Master of the Household, they are amongst the most important officials in Her Majesty's service.

The Privy Purse is that part of the financial provision made by Parliament at the beginning of each reign that is specifically devoted to the personal expenses of the Sovereign. The total annual allowance is called the Civil List and is made up of Her Majesty's Privy Purse, salaries of Her Majesty's Household, expenses of Her Majesty's Household, Royal Bounty, alms, and special services. The revenues of the Duchy of Lancaster belong personally to the Queen but the revenues of the Crown lands, amounting to more than double the total of the Civil List, are surrendered to the Exchequer. This surrender was first made by George III in 1783, when the loss of the American colonies had brought the country near to bankruptcy, but it was part of a process which began with William and Mary in 1689 and continued into the nineteenth century, by which less and less of the revenues of the country passed directly to the Monarch. In the seventeenth century the King had the disposal of all revenue and was responsible for payments to the Navy, the Army, the Civil Service, and all the other necessary public charges. By the time Queen Victoria came to the throne the change of this system had been gradually completed and the Sovereign received a fixed annual payment.

It remains to mention those offices of the Royal Household that, with the passage of time, have become extinct or been merged with other offices. James I, during whose reign many of the most splendid Court entertainments were given, created the office of Master of the Ceremonies, who wore a medal bearing an emblem of peace on one side and an emblem of war on the other. The duties were exclusively devoted to "dispensing the civilities of the Crown" to the

Corps Diplomatique and to foreigners of distinction. In 1920 the more rational title of Marshal of the Diplomatic Corps was conferred on the holder of this office. A Master of the Revels was needed in the days when the Tudor and Stuart monarchs delighted in the custom of Court performances of masques, plays, operas, and ballets. The Lord Chamberlain's present connexions with the theatre may be traced to this office.

The care of the Sovereign's ceremonial robes has resulted in the creation and merging of a number of offices. The oldest of these was that of the Groom of the Stole. In the time of Charles II this became the Mastership of the Great Wardrobe in charge of the King's Great Wardrobe which was housed in Wardrobe Place, still to be seen in the City of London. Under Edward VII the bearer of the office became Gentleman Usher of the Robes, under Edward VIII Master of the Robes and under George VI Groom of the Robes. Many writers have lamented the passing of the Royal Herb Strewer and her six maids, who scattered sweet herbs and flowers before the Sovereign during the procession from Westminster Hall to the Abbey. Their last appearance was made at the coronation of George IV, a monarch of whom Sir Max Beerbohm said that " he was implected with a passion for dress ", when their Regency gowns of white muslin with flowered ornaments were amongst the most charming of the dresses of that ornate occasion. The same coronation was marked by the last appearance of the King's Champion. This service, hereditary in the family of Dymoke, had been performed for nearly five hundred years and it is a cause of satisfaction that the tradition is partly kept alive by the appointment of the Champion to be Standard Bearer of England.

6. *The Great Officers of State*

W HEN preparations are on foot for the crowning of a monarch everyone is reminded of the existence of the Great Officers of State. Some of their offices exist at times other than coronations, a few of them with duties of the highest importance, but it is only on the occasions of the most solemn ceremonies of State that this group of officers, far older and at one time far more powerful than the Cabinet, achieves a faint shadow of its ancient splendour. There is no more certain way to capture some of the atmosphere of Plantagenet England than to repeat these imposing names—The Lord High Steward, the Lord High Chancellor, the Lord High Treasurer, the Lord President of the Council, the Lord Privy Seal, the Lord Great Chamberlain, the Lord High Constable, the Earl Marshal, the Lord High Admiral—and no better way to gain some understanding of the hierarchy of power from the eleventh to the fourteenth centuries than to pause and consider these nine great officers and their duties.

The Lord High Steward ranks as the first of the Great Officers of State. Under the Norman and Plantagenet kings and especially with such holders of the office as Simon de Montfort and John of Gaunt, the Steward claimed to be the second personage in the realm and the supreme judge in Parliament. The last permanent Steward was Henry IV's son, the Duke of Clarence. After his death the dangerous possibilities of the power of this official led to the practice of appointing a non-hereditary Lord High Steward only for specific occasions. A nobleman of great rank is appointed for each coronation and the Lord Chancellor of the day is elevated, when necessary, to preside at the trial of a peer in Parliament. Many of the Lord High Steward's ceremonial duties have vanished with the banquet in Westminster Hall. His right to follow the precedent of John of Gaunt to hear and determine the claims to perform coronation services has now been placed in commission. But he still has the privilege of performing one of the noblest duties at the coronation, that of bearing the Crown of St. Edward on a velvet cushion.

The judicial powers of the Lord High Steward at the trial of a peer vary according to whether the trial takes place during the sitting of Parliament or during the recess. During a session of Parliament the peers are both triers and judges, and the accused is thus tried by his peers or equals, in accordance with the right clearly expressed in Magna Carta. The Steward then acts only as the chairman of the court and gives his vote with the other lords. During a recess, however, the trial is held in the Court of the Lord High Steward. He is the judge, decides all questions of law but has no right to vote on the issue of guilty or not guilty. Trials before the Steward's Court are seldom held. In the seventeenth century there was a danger that a decision acceptable to the Sovereign would be obtained by summoning only a limited number of peers. A trial during a session of the House of Lords could be attended by all the peers, a right which was upheld by the Treason Act of William III. On the occasions of a trial in the House of Lords the Steward is addressed as "His Grace", he has a rod of office and the commission appointing him is dissolved by breaking the rod.

The position of the Lord High Chancellor, the second of the Great Officers of State, is very different from that of the

Steward. Not only is his office still alive but its power has grown, especially with the amalgamation of the duties of the Lord Keeper. For the origin of the office inquiry must be made far back into the functioning of government in the Roman Empire. The *cancellarii* were clerks devoted to notarial duties in the Roman courts of justice. Their value in an ordered community was such that, in course of time, they were to be found amongst most of the peoples who were once under the sway of Rome. Edward the Confessor, who was strongly influenced by the highly organized Court of the Dukes of Normandy, first introduced from France the office of Chancellor when he copied their practice of sealing instead of signing documents. It was inevitable that, at a time when literacy was almost confined to the clergy, the Chancellor should be a cleric. So he continued to be under the Norman kings. He combined the functions of the King's chaplain, private secretary, and keeper of the royal seal. Gradually the Chancellor and his staff of clerks undertook the whole clerical work of the Royal Household, which in those days meant the central machine of government. All petitions addressed to the Sovereign passed through his hands, thus giving rise to his powerful judicial position. Nothing can be more indicative of the tendency of this office to attract power to itself than the fact that, in the House of Lords, where the Lord Chancellor is now prolocutor, comparable to the Speaker in the House of Commons, he was originally an official of the House, present in the exercise of his duties but with no power to vote.

Today the Lord Chancellor is the highest judicial officer in England, the highest civil subject outside the Royal Family, taking precedence immediately after the Archbishop of Canterbury. He is the guardian of the Great Seal of the United Kingdom. He is a privy councillor, a member of the

The procession of the Lord Chancellor from Westminster Abbey to the House of Lords following the traditional service at the Abbey to mark the reopening of the Law Courts

John, twelfth Earl of Erroll, Lord High Constable of Scotland in 1685

The Lancaster Herald reading the Proclamation of the Accession of Queen Elizabeth I
at Charing Cross

government in office, usually a peer and a Cabinet Minister. He has special jurisdiction over charities and trusts, is the guardian of minors in the care of the Courts and of idiots and lunatics, is the visitor of royal foundations and the patron of all ecclesiastical livings in the gift of the Crown. He is unable to leave the country without the consent of the Sovereign. Objections have been raised to his political affiliations but these have been partly met by the removal of many of his judicial functions to the High Court of Justice. But he still presides over the hearing of appeals in the House of Lords and is the adviser of the Crown in the appointment of all judges, except the Lord Chief Justice. As the head of the law he acts in England alone, but as the Great Officer of State in charge of the seal he is supreme in the United Kingdom, one of the provisions of the Act of Union, 1707, being the appointment of one great seal for the whole country. The Great Seal of England, affixed on solemn occasions to documents expressing the pleasure of the Sovereign, was originally in the keeping of the Chancellor. As the holder of the office was usually an ecclesiastic and had other duties to perform, the personal custody of the seal came to be granted to another great officer called the Lord Keeper of the Great Seal. This officer was appointed by letters patent, whereas the Lord Chancellor held his office by the delivery of the seal. When the office of Lord Keeper was held by Sir Nicholas Bacon in the reign of Queen Elizabeth I its status was fixed by a special Act of Parliament which declared his equality with the Lord Chancellor. The possibility of rivalry between these two powerful officers was avoided by the practice of allowing the Lord Keeper to succeed to the Chancellorship. The last Lord Keeper was Sir Robert Henley, who was made Lord Chancellor on the accession of George III.

In the Chancellor's day-to-day functions in the House of Lords are to be found many of the interesting peculiarities which give life to traditional customs. His duties are frequently—and correctly—likened to those of the Speaker, but it would be a mistake to regard them as identical. The Lord Chancellor sits upon the woolsack, which is not strictly within the House of Lords. This "throne" with so homely a name is a large square cushion of wool, without back or arms, covered with red cloth. There is a tradition that it was first placed in the House of Lords in the time of Edward III, to emphasize the importance of the wool trade of England. But the first reference to the woolsack as the seat of the Lord Chancellor occurs in the reign of Henry VIII. Then woolsacks were used for all the officers of the House but for many years now it has been the privileged seat of the Lord Chancellor as prolocutor of the House of Lords.

The Lord Chancellor takes part in debates (but only by advancing from the woolsack to his place as a peer), has the right to vote, but does so from the woolsack, not by entering the division lobbies, has no power to call upon one debater in preference to another and cannot rule on points of order, in all of which particulars the opposite is true of the Speaker. In the House of Commons all debaters address the Speaker, in the House of Lords they commence "My Lords", thus addressing the whole House and not the Chancellor alone. These small differences may seem to place him in a slightly less eminent position than the Speaker, but it must be remembered that he has additional judicial, political, and chancery duties which make his office one of great power over a wide field. Blackstone said that in the old days the Chancellor "became keeper of the King's conscience". The modern holder of the office would not claim this remarkable distinction but there is no doubt that he is now the greatest of the Great Officers of State.

The Lord High Treasurer, the third of these officers, has ceased to exist except in so far as traces of his functions can be found in those of the First Lord of the Treasury, itself a sinecure post. In 1216, when the office of Lord High Treasurer was created, there were two duties—to guard the King's treasure at Winchester and to oversee the collection of the national revenue. The power of the Treasurer was at its height when there was no distinction between the national revenue and the Sovereign's income. But during the sixteenth and seventeenth centuries his absolute authority in financial matters was challenged by the creation of a secretary of the Treasury, and in the eighteenth century, as the democratic principle prevailed of ear-marking portions of the national revenue for State rather than for royal purposes, his position ceased to be necessary. The last Lord High Treasurer was the Duke of Shrewsbury, who resigned the post in 1714. Since then the duties of the office have been administered by a board, consisting of a First Lord, a Chancellor, and four or more Junior Lords. These are now all political appointments; the board never meets and the First Lord is a post without duties, usually held by the Prime Minister of the day.

The fourth Great Officer, the Lord President of the Council, occupies a position of much more recent origin than his three superiors. The Privy Council, over which he presides, is one of the oldest portions of the machinery of English government, but from the time of the Normans to that of the Stuarts its multifarious and frequently changing duties were controlled by the Lord Chancellor or the Lord Keeper. Gradually most of the Council's judicial and financial duties were given to other bodies and the advisory functions of the *concilium regis* became its pre-eminent activity. With the failure of the early Stuart kings to obtain absolute power came a period of complete impotence for the Council and the total abolition of its much feared department known as the Court of Star Chamber. But Charles II revived the Council, at the same time setting in motion the train of events which led to the formation of the Cabinet, which is the true Privy Council of the present day. In 1679 the office of Lord President, first tried on a temporary basis by Charles I, was made permanent. Today the holder is usually a member of the House of Lords and a Cabinet Minister with very limited departmental duties. The correct name of the Council is the Lords and others of Her Majesty's Most Honourable Privy Council. The members are addressed as "Right Honourable" and wear a State uniform of blue and gold with white breeches. Meetings of the whole Council are held very rarely—always at the beginning of a new reign or when the reigning Sovereign announces his or her marriage. In the former case it is strictly the Accession Council, a much more ancient body than the Privy Council.

Many of the former functions of the Privy Council are now carried out by separate ministries and it seems to be a feature of British constitutional government that departments which began as committees of the Privy Council become separate ministries as their importance increases. Examples of this tendency are the Ministries of Agriculture and Education and the Board of Trade. Of the functions remaining to the Privy Council two are of considerable importance, one administrative, the other judicial. The first depends upon powers specifically granted by Act of Parliament by which a committee of the Council may draw up Orders in Council enumerating the departmental details of a general measure, thus relieving Parliament of the necessity of enacting long and intricate legislation. The judicial function is exercised through the judicial committee of the Council, consisting of the highest judges in the land. Special leave to appeal to this committee must be obtained. Its proceedings are confined to certain categories of appeal cases—from ecclesiastical courts, consular and prize courts, vice-admiralty courts abroad, and some others.

The Lord Privy Seal, the fifth Great Officer of State, has been more fortunate than the Lord Keeper of the Great Seal in that his office still exists, albeit shorn of much of its original purpose. In the fourteenth century Parliament wished to have a check on the issue of public money and to prevent the use of the Great Seal by the Sovereign without any intermediary except the Lord Chancellor. The Privy Seal was therefore introduced, occupying a position between the Great Seal and the signet. Its authority was of a dual nature. It was a warrant to the Lord Chancellor to affix the Great Seal to such charters as must necessarily pass the Great Seal and it was also the authority needed for the issue of money from the Exchequer. Its use grew to such an extent that until the passing of the Great Seal Act in 1884 all letters patent conferring any dignity, office, monopoly, franchise, or other privilege were always passed under the Privy Seal before passing the Great Seal. The officer placed in charge of this vital safeguard was originally called the Keeper of the Privy Seal. By the reign of Edward III the holder of the office had become a Minister of State. Until 1537 he was always an ecclesiastic but is now usually a temporal lord and a member of the Cabinet without department duties.

As there has been mention of the two seals and the signet it remains to record the fourth method of transmitting the commands of the Sovereign—by means of the Royal Sign

Manual. This is the autograph signature of the Monarch by which he expresses his pleasure, either by order, commission, or warrant. It can be used either as an executive act, for instance an appointment to office, or as authority for affixing the Great Seal. The document must be counter-signed by a Principal Secretary of State. The Sign Manual is used to give power to make or ratify treaties. If the Monarch, through ill health, is unable to sign, powerful safeguards are introduced. George IV was permitted to use a stamp but he had to express his consent every time it was used and this was attested by a confidential servant and by several officers of State.

The Lord Great Chamberlain, the sixth Great Officer of State, is the holder of an hereditary position of great anti-quity. In 1133 the office was granted to the father of the first Earl of Oxford. It is now vested in a number of descendants of female heirs, who exercise its functions altern-ately reign by reign. In the chapter on the Royal House-hold reference has been made to the tendency of these here-ditary offices to become divorced from the duties originally associated with them. The office of Lord Great Chamberlain is an example of this procedure, with the Lord Chamberlain succeeding to the routine duties, leaving only the great ceremonial events to be carried out by the holder of the more ancient position. In normal times the Lord Great Cham-berlain's duties are concerned principally with the Palace of Westminster and especially with the House of Lords.

He is the nominal head of all authority in the Palace and exercises a complete authority when the Houses are not sitting. When the Sovereign opens Parliament in person he is responsible for the arrangements. He has the right to select the peer who is to carry the Sword of State and he himself walks in the procession on the Sovereign's right hand.

He has duties at the introduction of peers into the House of Lords on their creation and at the homage of bishops after their consecration. At the coronation he is one of the most important of the lay persons who perform portions of the ceremony. He still presents before the Court of Claims his ancient right to assist in dressing the King on the morning of the coronation. In the ceremony itself he stands on the left side of the Sovereign and fastens the clasp of the Imperial Mantle and girds on the Sword of State. Queen Victoria recorded how "the Dalmatic Robe was clasped round me by the Lord Great Chamberlain".

The seventh great office of State is that of the Lord High Constable. It was once a service of grand serjeanty of the earldom of Hereford. Through the female line it descended to the Dukes of Buckingham and on the attainder of the third Duke in the reign of Henry VIII it became merged in the Crown. It is possible that the abolition of its powers was due to the realization of the potential danger of allowing anyone to combine in one person the duties of commander of the royal armies, Master of the Horse, joint president of the Court of Chivalry and the administrator of martial law. Since the early sixteenth century the office has been brought into existence only temporarily for each coronation. The Lord High Constable accompanies the Earl Marshal in the procession and during the ceremony, and assists in the reception of the Regalia from the ecclesiastics who bear it into the Abbey. As long as the service of King's Champion was performed he shared with the Earl Marshal the privilege of riding into Westminster Hall with the Champion.

The eighth of the Great Officers of State is the Earl Marshal, whose functions in charge of all State ceremonial are still of considerable importance. The office, which is hereditary, has been held since 1672 by the Dukes of Norfolk, but it is of much greater antiquity and was previously held by other noble families. In feudal days the office of Marshal was closely connected with that of Constable, being in command of the army under the Constable, superseding that officer as Master of the Horse in the royal palace and exercising with him joint jurisdiction in the Court of Chivalry. It follows that the Earl Marshal plays an essential part in coronations, royal marriages, and funerals. With the Constable he rode into Westminster Hall with the Champion at the coronation banquet. The symbol of his office from Norman times has been a baton of gold tipped with ivory. The Duke bears crossed batons behind his shield and has the right to append the letters "E.M." to his signature.

Today the Earl Marshal is most widely known as the head of the College of Arms, the corporation of Heralds which controls grants of arms and has duties at all accessions, proclamations, coronations, and other royal ceremonies. The thirteen officers of arms are appointed at the discretion of the Earl Marshal and consist of Garter Principal King of Arms, two other Kings of Arms, six Heralds, and four Pursuivants. Their original functions were to act as messengers of kings, princes, and the great barons, and through their knowledge of armory to identify the nobles slain in battle. They wore splendid liveries bearing the arms of their master, which gave them immunity from injury or insult. The College was founded by Richard III and the Heralds still wear the loose tabard of arms associated with the days of their foundation. After the reign of Henry VI the College began to make a regular series of grants of arms and to claim that new arms were not valid unless assigned by the heralds. Their virtual monopoly was created by the willingness of people unversed in these intricate matters to apply to them as experts. In the eighteenth century they

fell into considerable professional disrepute but with the rise
of archæological studies their scholarship improved greatly.
There are no Colleges of Heralds in Scotland or Ireland but
offices of arms are presided over by Lyon King of Arms and
Ulster King of Arms, respectively.

The ninth of the great offices of State is that of the Lord
High Admiral. This officer, under whom the King's ships
gradually developed into the most powerful navy in the
world, was first appointed, but on a temporary basis only,
in 1360. The permanent appointment of a Lord Admiral
dates from 1406. One of the most successful of the Admirals
was James, Duke of York, who kept the office in his own
hands when he came to the throne as James II. The control
of the Royal Navy being thus maintained by an unpopular
monarch it was natural that the Revolution of 1688 caused
the office virtually to disappear. Since the reign of William
and Mary it has been in commission, except for the short
periods during which it was held by Prince George of
Denmark (1701–9) and the Duke of Clarence (1827–8).
The full title of the Lords of the Admiralty is the Commissioners for executing the office of High Admiral of the
United Kingdom. The First Lord is an important political
appointment and the principal professional officer is the
First Sea Lord. The Lord High Admiral, when he was in
executive command of a fleet, had the right to fly the royal
standard. At other times he used the Admiralty flag, a
gold anchor and cable on a red field, which is still flown
today by the Lords of Admiralty.

The kingdom of Scotland possessed great offices of State
equal in power and antiquity to those of England. One of
these, the office of Lord High Constable of Scotland, is
hereditary in the family of Erroll and still carries many
reminders of its ancient splendour. As in France, the Lord

High Constable was Commander-in-Chief of the Army and the highest martial judge. The Earl Marischal was his second-in-command. The Constable also had the duty of guarding the Sovereign's person on ceremonial occasions in Scotland and the permanent duty of maintaining law and order and judging cases of disorder within the verge of the Court. Order was enforced by the Lord High Constable's Doorward Guard of Partizans, a body roughly equivalent to the Yeomen of the Guard in England. This guard was in existence before 1300 and is probably the oldest royal guard still surviving in Britain, though today it is reduced by expense to a single token Doorward, who wears the badge of the Lord High Constable on his arm and is posted in the guard's traditional place at the foot of the Grand Staircase on ceremonial occasions at Holyroodhouse. But none of these traditions and customs is more powerful as a link with the past than the Lord High Constable's practice of maintaining a private officer-of-arms called Slains Pursuivant, who wears a tabard of the Constable's arms. Here is an example of the original function of the Heralds as privileged officers of the great noblemen, dating from before 1404 and still in existence five hundred and fifty years later.

7. *Accessions and Proclamations*

"THE King is dead. Long live the King!" The King cannot die. There is unbroken continuity in the succession to the throne, proved by the immediate transfer of the royal authority to a different person. The moment in which a king dies, "sad and not joyful" as Evelyn wrote when he recorded the death of Charles II, is also the moment in which his successor, surrounded by the well-wishing of his subjects, commences his reign. The atmosphere of this solemn occasion may vary from the almost hysterical grief of James II to the quiet dignity and composure of the young Queen Victoria, who, when she was awakened at six in the morning with the news that the Archbishop of Canterbury and the Lord Chamberlain wished to see her, got out of bed and went into her sitting-room, only in her dressing-gown, and received them alone. But whatever may be the personal reactions and however strong may be the feelings of sorrow, there must always be on such occasions a sense of the solemn assumption of sacred duties. Victoria spoke for all monarchs when she said, "Since it has pleased Providence to place me in this station, I shall do my utmost to fulfil my duty towards my country." The knowledge of being set apart for a special task is already apparent in the words "to place me in this station", and the events that crowd upon the Sovereign in the succeeding hours do everything to heighten the sense of dedication and loneliness.

For the moment, the change is not yet absolute. The English monarchy is a remarkable compromise. Its hereditary and symbolic elements are strong but it does not divest itself of all traces of an elective system. So, while the continuity of the monarchy is symbolized by the fact that the royal standard is never flown at half-mast, the necessity that the Sovereign should be accepted by his people is expressed by the absence of the royal arms from the *Court Circular* until after the Accession Council has met. This Council is an assembly of almost fabulous antiquity, older than Parliament, older even than the Privy Council, with which it is often confused. Its traditions lead back to the Witan, a group of delegates by which government was maintained under the Saxon kings. It is the representative body of the three estates of the kingdom, consisting of the Lords Spiritual and Temporal, the late king's Privy Council, other principal gentlemen of quality, the Lord Mayor, and Aldermen of the City of London. This grand Council of the nation is called into existence once in every reign to make the declaration that the new Sovereign is the true heir under the Act of Settlement. Only when this declaration has been made does the Sovereign hold his first Privy Council, when the leaders of Church and State make solemn avowal of their fidelity to their new Monarch. On the same occasion the Sovereign gives the promise, required by the Act of Union of Scotland, to safeguard the ecclesiastical settlement made in 1707. It is at this stage that the confusion between the Accession Council and the Privy Council probably occurs, because the Accession is proclaimed, not by order of the older assembly, but by the Privy Council as the more formally constituted body.

This proclamation of the accession of the Sovereign is the one event which permits of a relaxation of the public mourning that is in force between the death and the funeral of the previous Monarch. On the day of proclamation all flags on public buildings are hoisted right up from eight until eleven in the morning. The first proclamation is made, usually by Garter King of Arms, at St. James's Palace. The Heralds, attended by the Serjeants-at-Arms, appear on the old brick balcony above Friary Court. When the trumpets have sounded a fanfare the proclamation is read in the presence of the Earl Marshal and the High Steward of Westminster. A forty-one gun salute is fired at ten-second intervals. A State procession is then formed in which the Heralds and other officials, with an escort of Household Cavalry, ride in closed carriages to repeat the proclamation three times—once at Charing Cross and twice within the boundaries of the City of London. The coachmen and footmen wear red cloaks and black silk hats trimmed with gold braid and black cockades. At Temple Bar, where the High Steward of Westminster leaves the procession, the Lord Mayor of London is waiting behind a velvet cord stretched across the road. A Pursuivant, attended by two trumpeters, advances to the barrier. The trumpeters sound thrice, the City Trumpeters reply and demand is made for admission into the City. The Pursuivant is conducted by the City Marshal to the Lord Mayor, to whom the Order in Council is presented. The Lord Mayor gives permission for the procession to pass into the City and the cavalcade moves on to Chancery Lane and the Royal Exchange, the places appointed for the reading of the proclamation. A feature of the ceremony at the Royal Exchange is that a guard of honour is mounted by pikemen of the Honourable Artillery Company.

London has no monopoly of this ceremony. The accession is proclaimed throughout the Commonwealth. At Windsor the proclamation is read three times, the ceremony at the castle being attended by the Military Knights of Windsor in their blue cloaks. At York the Lord Mayor, standing on the steps of the Mansion House, drinks the health of the Sovereign from a gold cup. At the proclamation of Elizabeth II at Manchester the toast was given, "The Queen, Duke of Lancaster". In Ceylon, the proclamation was read in three languages, English, Sinhalese, and Tamil. At Canberra the Queen was proclaimed as "supreme liege lady in and over the Commonwealth of Australia". Everywhere, from small county towns to great capital cities, the British people make formal acknowledgment of the tradition by which the succession of Sovereign to Sovereign is the symbol of the continuing life of the nation and the Commonwealth. It is proper that this day is commemorated by a Form of Prayer with Thanksgiving to be used yearly on the day of the accession of the reigning Monarch.

Reference will be made to the lengthy interval that is now necessary between the accession and the coronation. This practice dates only from the reign of George III but the increasingly personal relations between the Sovereign and the constituent members of the Commonwealth give a new validity to the delay. In the case of Elizabeth II the coronation was proclaimed on 7th June, 1952, four months after the proclamation of her accession and twelve months before the coronation. The ceremony of the proclamation follows the same ritual as that on the occasion of the accession, with its four readings by the Heralds, except that, as the period of the general mourning has ended, the procession is a little more elaborate. On the previous day Queen Elizabeth held a Coronation Council and signed the proclamation "Declaring Her Majesty's Pleasure touching Her Royal Coronation and the Solemnity thereof". This document confirms the date of the coronation and sets out the names of the members of the Court of Claims. As it is read, four times by four Heralds, amidst the jingle of harness, the stamping of horses, and the excited comments of the spectators, one fact emerges above all others. This is no ordinary event that is being announced; it is a solemn ceremonial to which are summoned "all Persons of what Rank or Quality whosoever they be, who are to do any Service at the time of Our Coronation and of this they or any of them are not to fail, as they will answer the contrary at their Perils, unless, upon Special Reasons by Ourself under Our Hand to be allowed, We shall dispense with any of their Services or Attendances".

8. The Coronation

THE group of symbolic ceremonies, inadequately known as the coronation, is the most significant of all the rituals by which the Monarch and his people are drawn into an imaginative act of unity. The French, who called the ceremony the Sacring of the King, described more accurately the rich and mysterious mingling of religious and secular rites in which anointing, crowning, and enthronization are indissoluble elements. The crown is not even by tradition the most important of the emblems with which the Monarch is invested. That distinction our ancestors would have granted to the sceptre, the most ancient symbol of power. But the instinct that has singled out the putting on of the crown as the one element by which the whole complex ceremony shall be named may be fundamentally right. When the Archbishop takes the crown to put it upon the Queen's head, he will speak no words of power and might. It is a crown of princely virtues, a symbol of divine grace, to be seen in "manifold fruit of good works". There could be no more fitting symbol of the place of the monarchy in a modern State—shorn of much of its ancient power but preserving more vitally than ever before the true attributes of kingship.

There are many who regret the long delay between the proclamation and the coronation—an interval that blunts the keen edge of the symbolism of the coronation. Before the eighteenth century it was usual to have an interval of

The Proclamation of the coronation date of Queen Elizabeth II being read by Garter King of Arms from the balcony of Friary Court, St. James's. On the left of Garter King of Arms is the Duke of Norfolk, hereditary Earl Marshal of England

A selection of the Crown Jewels. The Sovereign's Orb, St. Edward's Crown, the Sceptre with Dove, and the Sceptre with Cross

A drawing by A. C. Pugin and J. Stephanoff of the coronation of George IV in 1821

weeks or at the most of a few months. George III allowed eleven months to elapse and so created a precedent which, from the changed nature of the Commonwealth, and the complications of modern life, is unlikely to be altered. At least a year is needed for all the arrangements to prepare Westminster Abbey for the ceremony, to consider the claims of service, and to bring together the representatives of the Dominions and the Colonies, and the distinguished visitors from other lands. Further, such an event, full of open-air pageantry, can take place only during the summer months. These delays cause a situation in which a monarch is crowned who has already been carrying out the duties of high office for more than a year. But the interval is absorbed into the complex ceremony by virtue of one event of high antiquity. This is the deliberations of the Court of Claims, a tribunal by which the rights are considered of those who believe they have hereditary or other privileges of rendering service to the Monarch at the coronation. Such a court existed at the time of the coronation of the Queen Consort, Eleanor of Provence, in 1236, but detailed records begin with the court held by John of Gaunt, as Lord High Steward of England, prior to the coronation of Richard II in 1377. Since the reign of Henry VII the powers of the court have been exercised by a body of Commissioners. It is unlikely that their task has ever been so difficult as it was before the coronation of Edward VII in 1902, when the long reign of Queen Victoria had caused a proliferation of the families having claims. These were examined with great care and many of the decisions then made have been used as precedents in succeeding courts.

The claims that the court considers are from those who maintain that they have the right to hold strictly hereditary offices and from those who hold estates that make them

F

ancient tenants on serjeanty. The most famous as well as
the oldest of the traditional services was the right of the
barons or portsmen of the Cinque Ports to carry the canopies
over the King and Queen, sixteen barons to each canopy,
during the procession between Westminster Hall and the
Abbey. This privilege was granted to them in return for
their invaluable services in the defence of the southern sea-
board of England before the days of the Royal Navy. The
picturesque procession was not revived after the coronation
of George IV in 1821 and the canopy with its silver bells,
borne through the streets by the portsmen in their sumptuous
uniforms of scarlet, purple, and gold, was seen no more.
Edward VII had the happy inspiration to give them a place
in the ceremony again by permitting them to stand outside
the screen in Westminster Abbey and to receive the standards
of the Empire as they are carried into the Abbey by their
bearers. The portsmen are more soberly but still most
beautifully dressed for their new office, in suits of black and
white silk covered with scarlet cloaks. As the Queen
enters the choir, the uplifted standards will be dipped.

The claims from ancient tenants in serjeanty are more
complicated. They are made by those who hold their land
in return for a service to be rendered to the King. With
the passage of time the obligation became a privilege and
was sometimes hotly contested between representatives of
different branches of the same family. Most of the duties
were connected with the King's Household and so it followed
that the services to be rendered were performed either at
the banquet or in the State procession. Amongst many
offices so distributed were those of Chief Butler, Grand
Almoner, Grand Carver, and Napier (in charge of the table
linen). The banquet and the procession were held for the
last time by George IV, so that many of the services have

since lapsed. Queen Victoria dispensed with them at her coronation, but without prejudice to their future performance.

The most picturesque of the serjeanty privileges was that of King's Champion, granted to the family of Dymoke of Scrivelsby from the year 1377 or earlier. It was remarkable that so direct a connexion with feudalism should have remained in practice into the nineteenth century but even then there were many who deeply regretted that the service was no longer performed. When the King had been elected, anointed and crowned, his Champion cast down the gauntlet three times and challenged to personal combat any who denied the royal honours. At the coronation of Edward VII a place was found for the Champion by permitting him to serve the office of bearing the Standard of England, a duty that he has fulfilled at each subsequent coronation. The only serjeanty service remaining in the coronation ceremony itself is the duty of providing and presenting a rich right-hand glove for the Monarch before the investiture with the two sceptres. This service is performed by the Duke of Newcastle.

The coronation service is a solemn ritual which has grown, expanded, and developed for over a thousand years. There are records of the coronation of Egferth, King of Mercia, in 785, but the earliest form of ritual is that associated with the name of Egbert, Archbishop of York from 734 to 766. Included in this Pontifical is the Mass for Kings on the Day of their Benediction, in which the ceremony of Unction, or "anointing to King", is the central feature. Regalia in a primitive form—the sceptre, staff and helmet, and the royal helmet with which the crowning was performed—are mentioned as essential to the ceremony. These take a larger place and are joined by the crown, the ring, and the sword in the second coronation order, which is attributed to the year 973 and has come to be called the Order of Ethelred II, although its connexion with that Monarch is uncertain. One of its most interesting additions is the ceremony for the coronation of a Queen Consort.

With the accession of Richard Cœur de Lion there are records of a type of ceremony bearing some relation to modern practice but the earliest reference to the mystery of anointing with holy oil or chrism is in the order of Henry I. The *Liber Regalis* of the coronation of Richard II in 1377 sets down for the wonder of posterity the details of the ritual of that beautiful occasion—details which were followed with little deviation for three hundred years and which remain powerful elements to the present day. The ritual—whether new or only recorded for the first time it is impossible to say— was drawn up by Nicholas Litlington, Abbot of Westminster. It contained the Royal Progress from the Tower to Westminster, the service of the King's Champion, the Homage of the Peers and other spectacular events by which public attention was focused on the coronation of the boy of whom Shakespeare said

> "Not all the water in the rough-rude seas,
>   Can wash the balm from an anointed King."

This great codex, sometimes called "The Book of the Royal Offices to be performed and observed according to the use of the Royal Church at Westminster", is still in the keeping of the Dean and Chapter of Westminster Abbey.

The next important development in the ceremony was the change of language from Latin to English, a reform which took two reigns to accomplish in its entirety. At the coronation of Queen Elizabeth I, 1558, the litany was read in English while the coronation order was rendered in Latin.

Her successor, James I, caused the rite to be translated into English for the first time for his coronation in 1603. This vernacular version was carefully revised in 1625 by William Laud, not yet Archbishop but then Sub-Dean of Westminster, for the coronation of Charles I. It was at the coronation of James II that substantial alterations were again made in the ceremonial. The King, anxious to surround himself with traditional magnificence, set the Heralds to search for precedents and induced Archbishop Sancroft to abridge the service so as to make it acceptable to a Roman Catholic Monarch. It was inevitable that, at the end of his short and troubled reign, this ritual was altered by his Protestant successors, William and Mary. The task of making this radical recension in four weeks was entrusted to Compton, Bishop of London. He went back to the Pontifical of Egbert, merging elements of this great Saxon rite with features from the *Liber Regalis* to form a service, which, with only minor changes, has been used at every coronation from 1689 to the present day. There have been criticisms that, by mingling the two rituals, much of the mystical element of the medieval service was lost for ever, but it is good to remember that the Bishop was the first to introduce the ceremony of presenting to the Sovereign a ceremonial copy of the Bible, "the most valuable thing that this world affords", and that it was he who, by altering the order so that the crowning comes in the place of climax, gave justification to the whole ceremony being called the coronation.

The Abbey Church of St. Peter at Westminster was built by Edward the Confessor to be, in the words of a later chronicler, "the head and crown of the realm". It was consecrated in 1065 and in the Charter of Foundation the King granted to the Benedictines of Westminster the privilege of guarding the national regalia. He applied to the

Pope for a Bull appointing the new church as the place of
regal consecration and coronation. From the time of the
last Saxon king to the present day every Monarch except two
has come to this church for the solemn ceremonies of
anointing, enthronization, and coronation. No other church
in the world can claim such a living tradition.

When the boy King, Henry III, succeeded King John in
1216, it was necessary for him to be crowned at Gloucester,
as the south-eastern part of England was in the hands of the
French. At the first opportunity the new King was crowned
a second time at Westminster, in the great Norman church
that he was to replace by the Gothic masterpiece which stands
today.

This strange King, a man of taste, culture, and piety,
yet lacking in the qualities necessary to make a ruler, whose
failures Dante summarized when he relegated him to the
limbo of ineffectual souls, left as his abiding monument his
devotion to the ideal of making a new resting-place of
incomparable beauty for the remains of St. Edward the
Confessor. The work was started in the year 1245 and
before the King's death in 1272 he had the satisfaction of
seeing the completion of the choir and the transepts. The
exceptional size of this first section, necessary for ceremonial
ritual, proves that Henry bore in mind the wishes of his pre-
decessor that the church should be the place of coronation
of the English kings. He caused to be constructed a superb
shrine for the body of King Edward, by the Italian artist
Peter Cosmati. He remembered the regalia, which, "for the
memory of posterity and for the dignity of the royal coronation", St. Edward had ordered to be preserved in his Abbey
Church. Henry's builders strengthened the crypt beneath
the Chapter House to be both the repository of the regalia
and the "Treasury of the King's Wardrobe". In 1303 the

royal treasure-house was burgled, but the regalia was not touched. Edward I immediately removed the Crown property to the Tower of London but allowed the regalia to remain in the keeping of the monks of Westminster. There they were safely kept, in the Chapel of the Pyx, until the Puritan Parliament of 1649 ordered that the regalia was "to be totally broken". When Charles II was restored to his throne, he gathered together the few pieces that had escaped this dreadful act of destruction and ordered Vyner, his goldsmith, to replace all that was lost. The new regalia was housed in the Tower of London, where it has been from then until this day.

Of all the symbols of kingship in these islands none is a more potent talisman than the Chair of St. Edward, enclosing the "Stone of Destiny" on which the kings of Scotland had been placed at their coronations for many centuries.

The practice of elevating the Monarch on a stone of ceremonial and probably religious significance is one of great antiquity in many parts of the world. In the British Isles there are at least three stones that are associated with the king-making rites of our early people—the King's Stone at Kingston in Surrey, the Stone of Destiny from Scone in Scotland, and the Stone of Tara, in Ireland. The known uses of some of these stones stretch back over a thousand years, with uncounted centuries of tradition, partly regal, partly priestly or druidical, lying in the shadows. The Stone of Scone is a rectangular block of sandstone with iron rings that may have been grasped during a prehistoric ceremonial rite, such as the taking of an oath of fealty. It was in 1296 that Edward I, during his short mastery of Scotland, removed the Stone from the Abbey of Scone and placed it in Westminster Abbey near the Shrine of Edward the Confessor. By this act he enriched the royal church built by his father with a relic to which traditions of a mystical nature were already clinging, but, at the same time, he inflamed bitter feelings amongst the people of Scotland which have lasted to this day.

The King's first intentions were to make a chair of bronze, in which the stone would be enclosed. But he changed his plans and ordered the chair to be made of oak, with a space for the stone beneath the seat. It was finished about the year 1300 and was painted, gilt, and set with glass enamels by Walter of Durham, the King's Painter. Its name, the Chair of St. Edward, was given to it in veneration of the founder of the Abbey. This remarkable relic has been used at every coronation since that of Edward II. Even Cromwell recognized the double significance of the stone within the chair and had it removed to Westminster Hall for his installation as Lord High Protector. Today it still exists, hallowed by six centuries of use by British Monarchs at the supreme moments when they are anointed, invested with the regal ornaments, and crowned. The chair has suffered serious mutilation and now bears almost no sign of its former splendid colours, but, as the shell of this strange block of sandstone, it is a symbol of the understanding of history that is a sense of the past and a sense of the future caught for a fleeting second in the present of each one of us.

When the people of Britain come to the crowning of their Sovereign, long and elaborate preparations are made in the Abbey, so that all who share in the ceremony, from the Monarch himself to the small boy who waits for half a day in the street to see the procession pass, may have renewed in them the certainty that here, on this day, individualities are submerged and all become part of a great company. In the document of regulations drawn up for the coronation of Charles I it is ordained that "there is a Stage to be set up four square close to ye foure high pillars between ye Quire and ye Altar. The stage is to be spread with Tapestrie and to have railes about it richly covered. It is also to have Staires out of ye Quire up to it, and down to ye Alter from it. There is a Throne of State to be erected on ye said Stage for the King. There is also another Chaire to be set below by ye Altar on ye South side for the King; a Faldstoole and cushens to pray at, and seats for ye Lds and Bps. There is also a Traverse to be sett up in S. Edward's Chapell for the King to disrobe himself in after ye ceremonies of his Coronation be ended". This "apparatus" is still prepared for every coronation. The stage is now called the Theatre and is the last surviving trace of the high scaffold on which the ancient kings were crowned, as part of the embedded tradition that the King should offer himself to be seen by the people—a tradition dating certainly from the crowning of the Emperors in Sancta Sophia at Constantinople, and from our own Saxon kings. It reached a pinnacle of elaboration at the coronation of Edward VI, when the stage was reached by a flight of twenty-two steps and the throne was covered by a canopy decorated with silver bells.

It is the privilege of each Monarch to present to the Abbey on the occasion of his coronation an embroidered frontal for the High Altar. Sometimes it has taken the form of a gift of precious fabric; on other occasions the altar has been vested in these hangings for the ceremony and a token gift has been made at the appropriate moment. George IV draped the altar in blue and gold brocade to a height of twelve feet. His namesake in 1911 gave a pair of cream-coloured frontals specially made to a pre-Reformation design. The first record of these beautiful gifts is also the most sumptuous. Henry III enriched his new Abbey Church with a magnificent frontal of *opus Anglicanum*, gold embroidery encrusted with pearls, garnets, and enamels, probably the work of Mabel of Bury St. Edmunds, a celebrated orphrey worker.

As the preparations for a coronation proceed, the regalia receives special attention. Amongst those objects of high symbolism, rightly called the Honours of England, are some which are of great antiquity, handed down from one Monarch to his successor for use at each coronation, and there are others which are made anew from time to time. Every Sovereign is crowned with St. Edward's Crown, is anointed with oil from the eagle-shaped Ampul poured into the Coronation Spoon, is girt with the Sword of State, touched with the Spurs of St. George, and invested with the Orb and the Sceptres. All these belong to the ancient regalia of the kings of England. They were destroyed in 1649 by order of the Puritan Parliament and were replaced at the Restoration of Charles II by new regalia bearing the old names—all except the beautiful Anointing Spoon, which was probably made for the coronation of Henry III in 1216, and the Ampul, which may only have been repaired by Vyner when he replaced the rest of the regalia in 1660. It is a reinforcement of what Henry James called "the respect for the mysteries of life" that the most sacramental act of the service of coronation should be performed with objects which have survived the holocausts of seven hundred years.

Of different and more personal natures are the Imperial Crown, worn by the sovereign in the final procession through the Abbey, and the Ring, placed by the Archbishop on the fourth finger of the King's right hand "as a sign of kingly dignity and the defence of the Catholic faith". Until 1549 this finger, the thumb counting as the first, was considered the wedding finger, so there was good reason for Mary and her sister, Elizabeth, to believe that they had assumed at their coronation the wedding ring of England.

During the late afternoon of the coronation eve the jewels are brought from the Wakefield Tower to Westminster in State coaches, with an escort of Household Cavalry. So the regalia returns to the Jerusalem Chamber in the Abbey Church of St. Peter in Westminster to fulfil the desire of Edward the Confessor that the priests should guard the national insignia. On the morning of the coronation a procession is marshalled in the Abbot's Courtyard. Led by the Abbey beadle bearing the mace come the King's Scholars of Westminster School, the choir of the Abbey and the children of the Chapel Royal, in surplices and scarlet cassocks and crimson and gold uniforms, the priests of the Chapel Royal in scarlet mantles, and then the Abbey clergy bearing the regalia. The Imperial Crown, the Ampul and the Anointing Spoon are deposited by the Dean upon the altars and then, as the whole body of singers chant the Litany, the procession moves down the nave to deliver St. Edward's Crown and the accompanying instruments of majesty into the keeping of the Lord Great Chamberlain.

The processions which were once an integral feature of the coronation have gradually been reduced to two—those in which the Sovereign is escorted from Buckingham Palace to Westminster Abbey and back to the Palace again. In the *Liber Regalis* it is ordained that the King on the day before his coronation shall ride bare-headed from the Tower of London through the City to his royal palace at Westminster.

The last Monarch to observe this ancient ritual of showing himself to his people was Charles II, a brave event of which Samuel Pepys recorded that "so glorious was the show with gold and silver, that we were not able to look at it, our eyes at last being so much overcome with it". Two other processions remained in use until 1821 and then were swept away by William IV. These were the processions on foot from Westminster Hall to the Abbey and back again to the Hall for the Coronation Banquet. Regret has sometimes been expressed that the full significance of all these functions was not realized by those who abandoned them. They were essential parts of the pre-coronation enthronement in West-minster Hall, a relic of the principle of secular election which remained within the complex structure of the coronation. The Monarch showed himself to his people before his election, and, when elected, walked to the Abbey on a raised platform, so that the acts of recognition performed in the Hall and the Abbey should be completed amongst the great mass of his subjects. Before him went the Great Officers of State bearing the regalia, the way for them all being prepared not by men of arms but by His Majesty's Herb Woman with her six maids, strewing the path with flowers.

In the modern processions the moment for which the great crowds wait patiently during the long hours is that in which the State Coach comes into view, drawn by eight Windsor greys, with four postilions and eight walking grooms. This is the superb rococo vehicle in which the new Sovereign is borne to the place of coronation. Designed by Sir William Chambers for George III, it is now nearly two hundred years old and, with its gilt carvings of tritons, dolphins, and palm trees, its panels painted by Cipriani, and its linings of scarlet velvet, it is the most sumptuous carriage still in royal use, a relic of an age of magnificent extravagance both in design and cost. In the coronation procession are seen many other beautiful State vehicles—the glass coaches in which ride other members of the Royal Family and the bright purple-lake landau built for Edward VII, which that expert on carriages, Sir Walter Gilbey, thought "the most graceful and regal vehicle ever built".

For the coronation a temporary annexe or vestibule is

constructed against the west front of the Abbey. Here the
Sovereign is received and the royal standard is flown while
the constituents are marshalled for that rich composite of
processions called the Great Proceeding. The first part
consists of the Royal Chaplains and other high ecclesiastics;
in the second are the representatives of the Orders of Chivalry
and the bearers of the standards of the British Empire.
When the Sovereign is a King and there is a Queen Consort
her procession forms the third section. The climax of the
Great Proceeding is the Sovereign's procession. Preceded
by the Kings of Arms and other Heralds, the bearers of the
regalia, the Lord Mayor of London carrying the crystal mace,
the Great Officers of State, and three bishops carrying the
paten, the chalice, and the Bible, the Sovereign enters the
Abbey between two files of Her Majesty's Body Guard of
the Honourable Corps of Gentlemen-at-Arms, armed with
their tall pole-axes. When Queen Elizabeth enters the nave,
there will be a great shout of "Vivat, Vivat Regina Eliza-
betha", from the boys of Westminster School. James II
granted to the King's Scholars the privilege of the Service of
Acclamation, a custom which has not only been continued
at every coronation but was extended by George IV to
include Town Boys as well. The Queen, in her crimson
Parliament Robe and Cap of Maintenance, will pass the
standards of the Empire, dipped in her honour, will proceed
through the choir and take her place at her Chair of Estate,
to the south of the High Altar.

There will be a moment of silence, as the Queen kneels
in prayer at her faldstool, in preparation for the supreme
ceremony which symbolizes the dual nature of the kingly
office—part priest, part soldier—which she assumed at her
accession and which on this day will be solemnly ratified.

There have been variations in the details of every coronation service but it is reasonable to suppose that all the great order of ritual will unfold itself again for the coronation of Queen Elizabeth II. First in that order is the Recognition, when the Queen stands in a position in which she can be seen by all the assembled company. Four times the Archbishop of Canterbury presents her to the people and asks if they are willing to do their homage and service, and four times the people signify their willingness and joy, the last cry of "God save Queen Elizabeth" being drowned in a fanfare of trumpets. This ceremony, always impressive, has taken on an added significance since the abolition of the secular enthronement in Westminster Hall. Then the lords who carry the regalia come to the High Altar and reverently pass the Honours of England into the keeping of the Church, so that they may come to the Queen as a trust from God. Only the four swords remain in the hands of noblemen— the Great Sword of State, Curtana or the Sword of Mercy, and the Swords of Temporal and Spiritual Justice. At this point in the service there have been several changes in the order. At the coronation of George IV, the King here took the oath, a worthy rearrangement by which the Sovereign's recognition by the people is followed by the solemn promise of constitutional government and the maintenance of the laws of God and the Protestant Reformed Religion. George VI was the first monarch to take the oath in the altered form necessitated by the Statute of Westminster.

In the first part of the Communion Service, which follows, there occurs one of the most moving examples of the power of tradition in these regal ceremonies. The reading from the Gospel is the famous passage from St. Matthew counselling the Pharisees to "render unto Caesar the things which are Caesar's". This passage has been read at every English coronation of which there is record from that of King Edgar the Peaceful in 973. After the Creed the normal order of the Communion Service is interrupted to place the sacring of the Monarch in this most hallowed setting. The first of these rites is the Anointing or Unction, not only first in temporal order but pre-eminent in its sacramental quality.

The Queen, divested of her Parliament robe and cap of State, and wearing a simple gown of crimson satin, a colour demanded by the most ancient traditions, takes her seat in St. Edward's Chair, while the choir sings Handel's great anthem, "Zadok the Priest", as it has been sung at every coronation from the time of George II. Four Knights of the Garter, in the blue velvet robes of their Order, hold a canopy of cloth of gold over the Queen's head, as a sign that the anointing is a mystery not to be lightly viewed. The Archbishop touches the Queen with holy oil or chrism, saying "so be you anointed, blessed and consecrated Queen over this People". This sacred rite of hallowing was formerly restricted to five monarchs in the world. Of these the Sovereign of England is the only one remaining in possession of her throne.

Now follows a stately order of vestments of ecclesiastical origin—the Colobium Sindonis, a tunic of white linen; the Supertunica, or St. Edward's Mantle; the Stole, or Armill; the Pallium Regale, or Imperial Mantle. These bear resemblances to the alb, the dalmatic, the stole, and the cope worn by a bishop and the ceremonies follow very closely those used for episcopal consecration. For Queen Victoria's coronation the Supertunica was skilfully adapted into a woman's garment, made of cloth of gold, edged with gold lace, and decorated with a design of pale green palm branches, pink roses, purple thistles, and green shamrock. It was lined throughout with rose-coloured silk. For practical reasons this order of ecclesiastical vesting is interrupted to allow the

Sovereign to be presented with the spurs and girded with the sword. This is the first introduction into the sacred ritual of the emblems of knighthood, sign of the dual nature of the kingly office, from which theorists of the Middle Ages derived many bitter arguments for and against the Sovereign's priestly authority. In the case of a king, the Lord Great Chamberlain touches his heels with the Golden Spurs of chivalry, but to Queen Elizabeth, as a Queen Regnant, they will be presented for her to touch them with her hand. The ceremony of the sword is long and complicated.

The Great Sword of State, made for the coronation of William and Mary in 1689, is much too large to be used for any purpose but to be borne aloft as an emblem of majesty. It is now removed from the theatre and is replaced by the Offering Sword, the superb jewelled arm made for George IV in 1821. This is laid upon the altar to be blessed and then is carried by the Archbishops and delivered into the Queen's right hand. The Lord Great Chamberlain fastens the sword to the royal girdle as the Archbishop of Canterbury proclaims the admonishment to "do justice, stop the growth of iniquity, protect the holy Church of God". The Queen now removes the sword, and, going to the altar, offers it there in its scabbard. The peer who first carried it has the duty of redeeming it for the sum of one hundred shillings, offered in a velvet bag. It is borne aloft naked during the rest of the ceremony.

The ceremonies in which the Queen is arrayed in the coronation vestments are completed with the investiture of the Armill and the Royal Robe, both garments decorated with silver eagles symbolizing dominion in the four corners of the world subject to the will of God. Seated in King Edward's Chair, in the full robes of office, the Queen receives the delivery of the Orb with the adjuration to remember

The Investiture of the Prince of Wales at Caernarvon Castle in 1911. King George V presents the Prince to the people at the King's Gate

An engraving from the painting by Sir George Hayter showing the scene in the Chapel Royal, St. James's, during the marriage in 1840 of Queen Victoria and Prince Albert

The wedding of Princess Elizabeth and the Duke of Edinburgh at Westminster Abbey, November 1947

"that the whole world is subject to the Power and Empire of Christ", and is invested with the Coronation Ring, "so you may be sealed with that Spirit of promise, which is the earnest of an heavenly inheritance". It is at this point in the ceremony that the ancient serjeanty service of the presentation of a rich glove embroidered with the arms of the Duke of Newcastle takes place. Originally this glove was scarlet but in recent coronations it has been made of white kid. As soon as it is placed on the Queen's hand the Archbishop delivers the two Sceptres, the Sceptre with the Cross into the Queen's right hand and that with the Dove into her left. This is the only occasion on which the Sovereign carries two sceptres and with this investiture of the rod and staff the central point of the old coronation service is reached. There is no more ancient symbol of power in the world than the tree from which these sceptres are descended.

Today the final majesty of kings is in their coronation and it is to the pageantry of that moment that the ceremony now moves. Pages in costumes of scarlet, buff and silver, sky-blue and silver, violet and white, carry coronets to peers engaged in formalities around the throne. The Dean of Westminster brings the crown from the altar, the Primate takes it from him and, as the Queen sits in St. Edward's Chair, the Crown of St. Edward is reverently placed upon her head. At once there is a great shout of "God Save the Queen", in which the boys of Westminster School lead the whole assembly, the peers and the peeresses assuming their coronets at the same instant. The Kings of Arms put on their heraldic crowns, and the thin, bright tones of the silver trumpets of the Royal Regalia cut through the repeated acclamations of thousands of voices as the fanfares ring in the vaulted roof. Outside, the bells can be heard and, heavy in the distance, the deep, resonant voices of the guns in St. James's Park and at the Tower. Queen Victoria thought it "a most beautiful impressive moment" and so it has always been to those who gather to see their Sovereign crowned.

The Presenting of the Bible is a calm ceremony, full of symbolism as deep as it is simple, drawing universal attention on this great day to the influence of the English Bible in the life of our people. The quietness with which it is carried out prepares the way for the solemn moment of the Great Benediction, a comprehensive blessing upon the Queen, the clergy and nobles assembled here, and upon all the people of the land, that they may "enjoy peace, plenty, and prosperity".

One rite remains, without which the intricate ceremonial would be incomplete. The Sovereign must be seated on high upon a throne of royal state, placed there by the hands of spiritual and temporal peers, in accordance with the ancient custom of the *levatio* by which the rulers of primitive peoples were lifted upon the shields of their warriors. The Queen moves from St. Edward's Chair to the raised theatre, where the Archbishops, the Earl Marshal and other noblemen raise her on to the throne. Then the Primate repeats the solemn exhortation, beginning "Stand firm, and hold fast from henceforth the seat and state of royal and imperial dignity, which is this day delivered unto you".

It is fitting that the Queen, anointed, crowned and enthroned, should now receive the homage of her people. This ceremony has been much reduced in length by the expedient of restricting its performance to the senior of each rank of the peerage—first the Archbishop of Canterbury on behalf of the lords spiritual, then the Princes of the Blood Royal, and, following in their order, a Duke, a Marquess, an Earl, a Viscount, and a Baron. As each makes his vows of fealty or homage the members of each order kneel bare-headed in their places. Then their representative touches the crown on Her Majesty's head and kisses her hand. The Westminster boys lead the congregation in the three-fold Biblical Salute and the solemnity of the Queen's coronation is ended.

There remains the conclusion of the Communion Service. The Queen relinquishes her Sceptres and passes through the Sanctuary to the steps of the Altar. The beautiful gesture of George II in removing his crown, symbolical of the putting off of human pride, has become an honoured tradition. The Queen kneels and offers bread and wine for the Communion. Then she makes her oblation of an altar cloth and an ingot of gold a pound weight and returns to her Chair of Estate. The Archbishops, the Dean of Westminster, and the Bishops who have taken part in the ceremony now communicate, before the Primate and the Dean administer the bread and the cup to the Queen.

For the Post-Communion the Queen puts on her Crown, takes the Sceptres in her hands again and returns to her throne on the dais. It is a short service of prayer ending with the pronouncing of the Benediction and the singing of the great *Te Deum*. In the meantime, the Queen, attended and accompanied as before, the four Swords being carried before her, descends from her throne crowned, and passes into St. Edward's Chapel. There is a pause in which the tension relaxes a little—but for a moment only.

The Yeomen of the Guard file into the Choir to line the processional way, the Canons of Westminster pass from the Chapel through the Abbey, followed by the Archbishops of York and Canterbury, walking in the shadow of the great silver crosses of their archdioceses. Then a fanfare rings through the Church and the Queen appears, wearing the Imperial

[99]

Crown and the Royal Robe of purple velvet, its noble train carried by eight pages and a peer. She holds the Sceptre and the Orb as she moves slowly from St. Edward's Chapel, through the Choir and the Nave, and out of the West Door of the Abbey Church.

When a King is crowned and there is a Queen Consort the ceremony of her coronation takes place after the Homage and before the second part of the Holy Communion. The service is short compared to that of the Monarch but it is of great antiquity and has suffered fewer alterations than the major rite. In substantially its present form this ceremony is at least a thousand years old.

Of the important elements of a coronation which have been allowed to lapse, reference has already been made to the Procession through the City from the Tower, the Enthronement in Westminster Hall, the Banquet and the service of the King's Champion. The suspended custom of the Royal Largesse has passed unregretted from the coronation order. During the Homage it was the duty of the Treasurer of the Royal Household to scatter medals of gold and silver, which were eagerly scrambled for by the congregation. At Queen Victoria's coronation the noise and confusion were the cause of considerable disturbance and everyone approved of the dignified change made by Edward VII. It was announced on the day of his coronation that the Royal Largesse would take the form of the gift of Osborne House to the nation.

9. The Investiture of The Prince of Wales

MOST of the great ceremonies of State are concerned with the kingdoms of England and Scotland, but there is at least one that brings the Principality of Wales into the full light of history. This is the creation of the Prince of Wales, an honour second only to that of the Sovereign.

The first Prince was Edward, the second son of Edward I. Legend has painted an attractive picture of the warrior king persuading the Welsh chieftains to accept as their prince one who was born in Wales, could speak no English and was of irreproachable character, and then presenting to them his own son, newly born at Caernarvon Castle. But it seems that this story was created to account for the uneasy peace which came to North Wales after the Statute of Wales, passed at Rhuddlan in 1284, the year of the young prince's birth. A few months later his elder brother, Alphonso, died and Edward became heir-apparent. In 1301, at the Parliament at Lincoln, his father created him Prince of Wales. Then, certainly, his position was used to help in the pacification of the warlike Welsh. The long tradition of investing the Prince of Wales with the robes and emblems of his dignity began with the investiture of Edward, the Black Prince, in 1343. The entail was declared to be "to him and his heirs the first-begotten sons of the kings of England". In spite of this clear pronouncement there have been at least two cases when the eldest surviving son has been created Prince of Wales—Henry VIII and Charles I both succeeded their deceased elder brothers. All these investitures took place in London, in the seventeenth century at the Palace of Whitehall following a ceremonial procession on the Thames when the Lord Mayor of London went out in his barge to greet the Prince. In the case of Prince Charles, in 1616, Chamberlain wrote that "our gallants flaunt it out in their greatest bravery at the Prince's Creation; which was performed on Monday at Whitehall, with all solemnity within doors; for the sharpness of the weather did not permit any public show". The Prince came bare-headed into the Great Hall, where James I sat enthroned, surrounded by "the whole State of the Realme in their Order". He made low obeisance to His Majesty three times and, after the third time, approached the King and knelt on a rich cushion. The Principal Secretary read the Letters Patent. At the words of investment the King put the robes upon him, girded on the sword, placed the rod in his hand and the ring on his finger, and set the cap and coronet on his head. The document of the Patent was handed to the King, who delivered it to the Prince, kissing him on both cheeks. At the putting on of the mantle and the delivery of the Patent, the trumpets and drums sounded.

It has always been a tradition that the heir apparent should be given the dignity of the Principality of Wales at an early age. The first Prince was seventeen, the Black Prince was thirteen, Henry and Charles, the sons of James I, were sixteen, the Duke of Windsor was seventeen, Henry VIII was only eleven. Less easy to trace are the customs relating to the insignia with which he is invested. The Black Prince received at the hands of his father a chaplet of gold made in the manner of a garland, a gold ring, and a silver verge, rod or sceptre. This open coronet is of much older origin than the single-arched crown the Prince wears as heir apparent. Other emblems were added at later creations and by the time Henry of Monmouth was invested by Henry IV it is believed that the five ensigns were in use— the mantle, the sword, the coronet, the gold ring, and the golden verge. When George I became reconciled with his son and created him Prince of Wales in 1714 it was stated that the coronet was the token of Principality and that the gold ring signified that the Prince must be a husband to his country and a father to her children.

In this century there have been several additions to the emblems of the Prince of Wales. Edward VII commanded the dragon to be incorporated in the Prince's armorial bearings. This was taken from the badge traditionally ascribed to Uther Pendragon, father of King Arthur, and certainly a warlike and magical symbol of extreme antiquity, brought to these islands from the East by the Romans. George V ordered a special standard to be prepared for the Prince of Wales, with the four lions of Llywelyn the Great on a shield of honour laid upon the shield of his arms as heir to the throne. But the most famous emblem connected with the Prince is one that has come down with the honour across the centuries and has lost the story of its origin in the passage of time. This is the badge of three ostrich feathers, with the motto *Ich Dien* ("I serve"). Camden, the Elizabethan historian, said that this was originally the crest of John, King of Bohemia, who was defeated and slain by the Black Prince at the Battle of Crécy. It was certainly used by the Black Prince as his badge "for Peace"—he had another badge "for War"—but there is no proof that it was ever the badge of the great Bohemian king. Today, when the feathers grouped in this manner are worn by every débutante, the badge of the Princes of Wales and of who knows what fierce warriors before them, has passed into the most decorous of general usages.

It was in 1911 that the investiture was revived with a splendour surpassing any of its predecessors and with several admirable features that were unique. Edward, the nineteenth Prince of Wales and the seventh of his name, was the first to be invested in his own principality; for the first time those in attendance on him were Welsh; for the first time a Prince of Wales addressed his people in their own language. These precedents were more than sufficient to make memorable the ceremony that took place in Caernarvon Castle on 13th July, 1911. Many of the famous castles of Wales were suggested as the site of the ceremony and Caernarvon was chosen, not only for its connexion with the legend of Edward I, but as the undoubted birthplace of the first Prince of Wales and as an impressive building suitable for such an act of ceremonial. There were two processions. The first to be received at the Water Gate by the Constable of the Castle was that of the Prince, escorted by a troop of Welsh Hussars and a troop of the Prince of Wales's Dragoon Guards. As the procession entered the Castle the Prince's banner as a Knight of the Garter was flown from the Chamberlain's Tower. A few moments later it was lowered and the royal standard was hoisted as the procession of the King and Queen arrived, with a Sovereign's escort of the Household Cavalry. The King's great procession of heralds, peers, sheriffs, lords-lieutenant and other distinguished people of Wales made its way round the walls to the open space near the Black Tower where three thrones had been set up. His Majesty took his seat on the central throne and commanded the Earl Marshal to direct Garter King of Arms to summon the Prince. In a riccote of crimson velvet, furred with ermine, and a crimson cap of estate with tassles of Venice gold, the Prince passed to the throne through an avenue of Welsh peers bearing the regalia. The Letters Patent were produced by Garter King of Arms and passed, by tradition, to the Lord Great Chamberlain, who handed them to the King, so that they would reach the Home Secretary, to whom fell the duty of reading them, from the Sovereign himself. At the appropriate moments in the recital, His Majesty invested the Prince with the mantle of purple velvet edged with gold lace, with the sword in its crimson scabbard, with the open circlet of gold, with the gold ring on the third finger, and with the verge made of gold mined in Wales. The Prince then did homage to the Principality of Wales and the Earldom of Chester with these words, "I, Edward, Prince of Wales, do become your liege man of life and limb, and of earthly worship and faith and truth. I will bear unto you to live and die against all manner of folks." The King kissed him on either cheek and the Prince of Wales, invested in accordance with the solemn and ancient ritual, took his seat on the third throne.

Then followed the popular ceremony of presenting the Prince to his people, based in part upon the tradition that Edward I had presented the infant Prince from Queen Eleanor's Gateway, but also, and more firmly, upon the ceremony of presentation which is an essential feature of the English coronation. The Arch Druid delivered an address on behalf of the Welsh people, to which the Prince replied in the same language. There was a religious service, before the great procession was re-formed and made its way to Queen Eleanor's Gate, the King's Gate, and the platform facing the bailey. At each of these places the King showed his son to the people as their invested Prince. The enthusiasm was tremendous as the crowds broke into singing the once popular anthem, "God Bless the Prince of Wales".

10. *Royal Christenings, Weddings, and Funerals*

THE christenings of royal children have not always been celebrated with public ceremony. The view that these are events private to the family has often prevailed. One of the exceptions was the christening of the Prince of Wales in 1842, when the celebrations were combined with an investiture of the King of Prussia with the Order of the Garter. The day began with a very elaborate service in St. George's Chapel, attended by foreign royalty, ambassadors, Cabinet Ministers, and other guests, all in full dress. Lady Lyttelton recorded the skill with which the Mistress of the Robes handed the child to the Archbishop of Canterbury and took him back again, avoiding the anticipated danger of the Prince snatching away the Primate's wig. This was followed by the investiture, by a lunch served in three parts and, in the evening, by a Grand Banquet in St. George's Hall. As a record of one day's activities at the Court, in which the principal figure was a lady whose confinement had taken place only two months before, this must be without parallel.

Royal weddings have always been occasions of great popular rejoicing, but they have not always been organized in ways which would permit these feelings to be fully expressed. The most popular royal wedding of the seventeenth century, that of Princess Elizabeth and the Count Frederick in 1613, was held in the tiny Chapel Royal at

Whitehall, so that none but the highest nobles were able to be present. Charles I was married by proxy in France, while the wedding of Charles II, charming as it must have been with his Portuguese bride in an English costume of rose-coloured silk, was performed with extreme discretion in the King's House at Portsmouth. In the eighteenth century the only royal wedding in which the public were encouraged to join was that of George III and Queen Charlotte, who were both married and crowned within the space of a fortnight. The wedding of Queen Victoria in 1840, strongly though it caught the general imagination—the bride and bridegroom both well-favoured in looks and still almost children—was held in the small and unostentatious Chapel Royal at St. James's Palace. Special arrangements had to be made to erect galleries of seats for distinguished guests in the courtyard outside. This desire of the Royal Family to preserve privacy at their weddings fitted well with Queen Victoria's dislike of ceremonies. She refused to allow the wedding of the Prince of Wales and Princess Alexandra to be held in London, and, as she grew older and became more attached to family celebrations, arranged the wedding of Princess Beatrice in 1885 at the simple parish church of Whippingham in the Isle of Wight. In the present century matters have been differently ordered. George VI, then Duke of York, was married to Lady Elizabeth Bowes-Lyon in Westminster Abbey in 1926. Twenty-one years later the same stately building, focus of national rather than family celebrations, was the setting of the marriage of Princess Elizabeth, now our Queen, and the Duke of Edinburgh.

The melancholy of our northern temperament investing our poetry and music with that "dying fall" which is amongst their most captivating graces, has inevitably found a rich field of expression in the mortality of kings. With Shakespeare we and our ancestors have cried,

> "For God's sake—let us sit upon the ground,
> And tell sad stories of the death of kings."

In the past our dead Sovereigns were taken to their graves with every mark of funeral pomp; today the ceremonies may be given a new simplicity but they have lost nothing of the ancient melancholy.

The passing of a Sovereign is announced by the tolling of the State bell of St. Paul's Cathedral. The King's Company of the Grenadier Guards assume the solemn office of guarding the body until the commencement of the lying-in-state, thus marking the intimate relationship between the throne and this select and chosen company of Household troops, a relationship which is brought to a fitting culmination when the King's Company colour is buried with the Monarch who presented it. A memorial salute of guns is fired at the Tower of London, one for each year of the Sovereign's life. In due time the body is taken, with all simplicity, to Westminster Hall, where among the stones which tell so much of this country's story, the people of Britain pass in a great stream of respect and affection. On the day appointed for the funeral the quiet homage is replaced by a great pageant of national mourning and remembrance as the body of the Sovereign is drawn by his sailors from Westminster to Paddington on the first part of the journey to the beautiful shrine at Windsor, where, since 1483, most of his ancestors have been buried. At the end of a short but impressive service, Garter King of Arms proclaims the style and titles of the dead King, the trophies of his achievements laid at the foot of his tomb.

The royal vault at Windsor is situated at some distance from the place in the choir where the coffin is lowered. There is a record that, after the burial of the Prince Consort, the attendants descended into the vault with lights and moved the bier and coffin along the narrow passage to the royal vault. A few years earlier, at the time of the death of Queen Adelaide, the question arose of the Sovereign's right of access to the royal vault, as it seemed that the Dean and Chapter claimed authority over it. An agreement was then made by which the fee paid for breaking the ground in no way affected the right of property held by the Crown over the royal vault. In 1862 Queen Victoria commenced the erection of the royal mausoleum in the grounds of Frogmore, a house in Windsor Home Park often occupied by George III and Queen Charlotte and later the home of the Duchess of Kent. It is a cruciform building, with an octagonal lantern, richly adorned with marbles and mosaics. Here Queen Victoria was buried in 1901.

On the occasion of the death of a Sovereign, the period of general mourning is proclaimed by the Earl Marshal and Court mourning is ordered by the Lord Chamberlain. The duration of the period for a king or queen is usually three months. The custom of placing wreaths on the coffin is comparatively modern. It did not come into general use until about 1870, its introduction coinciding with the disappearance of the practice of throwing a sprig of rosemary into the grave. When Queen Victoria became a widow she modified the conventional English widow's cap by introducing a Mary Stuart point over the centre of the forehead. This picturesque variation became fashionable, not only in England but also amongst royal widows abroad.

In the Middle Ages the death of the Sovereign was announced by a "Death Crier" or "Death Watch" who went through the streets tolling a bell and proclaiming the melancholy announcement. In London he was attended by the brotherhood or guild of the Holy Souls, each carrying a lighted candle. It was the practice for a waxen effigy to be made of the Monarch. This figure, in regal robes, was exposed on the catafalque under an elaborate canopy at the crossing in Westminster Abbey, that is, the very spot on which the Sovereign had been crowned. The effigies were astonishing likenesses. The head of the figure of Henry VII, which still exists in the Abbey, seems to have been taken from a death mask. At the interment of Henry VIII, his waxen image was carried in a chair all the way to Windsor. It was followed by a thousand noblemen on horseback, all the horses being draped in black velvet. The crowned figure of Queen Elizabeth carried at her funeral and the effigy on her tomb were both taken from her death mask. The placing of these figures at the crossing in the Abbey was not the only symbolism connecting the coronation and the obsequies. Edward II was buried in the linen shirt and coif which he wore at his consecration and his tunic and gloves were also buried with him. The robes in which kings were anointed were preserved for their burial. In their end was their beginning. If today no *memento mori* is found necessary, loyalty still contrives an expression of solemn magnificence to accompany the lost leader to the edge of the tomb. There all must draw back in silence.

> "The heart ran o'er
> With silent worship of the great of old!—
> The dead, but sceptred sovereigns, who still rule
> Our spirits from their urns."

11. Peerage, Knighthood, and the Orders of Chivalry

To many observers of the egalitarian tendencies of the past two hundred years it must seem that the existence of peerage and knighthood, carrying with it the principle of ennobled blood, is as far from the spirit of our times as the orders of chivalry with their fantastic codes of honour devised in the interests of an exclusive class.

But it is proper to remember that, in Britain, all these remnants of feudalism have been adapted in a supple manner to the changes of society, thus making them not only different from their own origins but totally unlike institutions of similar name in other countries. The peers of today can be traced historically to the Norman barons, the tenants-in-chief amongst whom William the Conqueror distributed land, the only source of wealth, in the form of manors. In return these tenants owed the Sovereign the service of attending the King's Court when it was held at the three great festivals of the Church. Within a century of the Conquest the principal barons had achieved the distinction of being summoned by name, all the smaller tenants being commanded by a general writ issued by the sheriff of their shire. The existence of two definite sections of the King's tenants was confirmed and codified in Magna Carta. The greater barons, summoned to their official duties by personal writ, were the direct ancestors of the peerages and came to be entitled to seats in the House of Lords. The other tenants-in-chief gradually accommodated themselves to a system by which they lost the right of personal service, became represented by two elected knights for each shire and at length joined forces with the citizens and burghers to form the House of Commons.

The peers summoned to the King's Courts of the twelfth and thirteenth centuries consisted of earls and barons, together with archbishops, bishops, and heads of ecclesiastical houses. The earls were barons with a special dignity added. So the peerage remained until 1337 when Edward III created his son Duke of Cornwall and gave him precedence over the rest of the peerage. The original intention may have been to restrict this great honour to members of the Royal Family but fifty years later Richard II created Robert de Vere Duke of Ireland for life, thus opening this title to those not of royal blood. The same nobleman was the first marquess. This title was imported from the Continent, as was that of viscount, which was added by Henry VI in 1440. During the four centuries from the Conquest to the death of Henry VI the principle of hereditary succession to a peerage was slowly accepted. The change followed the recognition that the duties of peerage were not burdensome necessities but privileges and opportunities of power. Those possessing the rights became anxious to preserve them for their descendants. The hereditary nature of the Crown itself was a precedent leading to the establishment of an hereditary peerage. But the duties of taking a leading part in the government of the country and the absence of any special privileges attaching to the children of a peer prevented the growth of an indolent class intent only on power-seeking. Such a development was a real danger in the reign of Henry VIII, when the dissolution of the monasteries transferred wealth and privileges to the temporal peers, but it was severely countered

Princess Elizabeth and the Duke of Edinburgh in the robes of the Order of the Garter after their investment at Windsor in 1948

In the Irish State Coach, the Queen drives in procession from Buckingham Palace to Westminster to open the new session of Parliament, November 1952

The Queen, with the Duke of Edinburgh, passing through the Royal Gallery of the House of Lords during her first State Opening of Parliament. Preceding her is Field-Marshal Earl Alexander of Tunis carrying the Sword of State

during the eighteenth century when it became the practice to ennoble men of proved experience in the conduct of affairs.

This practice emphasized the difference between English and continental peerage. Unlike a nobleman in France and Germany, an English peer was not a member of a privileged caste but a holder for life of offices entitling him to exercise legislative and judicial powers. These powers could only be used in conjunction with his fellow peers assembled in Parliament and subject to the constantly increasing check of the House of Commons.

The origin of knighthood is lost in the obscurity of Frankish and Teutonic history. The German tribes in the days of Tacitus are known to have celebrated the admission of young men into the ranks of their warriors with primitive ceremonies. The Crusades gave a great impetus to the conception of chivalry. Military orders were established bearing a strong analogy to the orders of priesthood. From these grew bodies of knights, obeying a supra-national authority and claiming a vocation partly religious and partly warlike. The survival in Britain alone of the title of knight bachelor acts as a reminder that not all knights were attached to the orders of chivalry. All over Europe in the Middle Ages armies were composed of small groups fighting under the pennons of knights. These leaders achieved their position by a long and arduous period of training as page, squire, and squire of the body. When his prowess had been proved beyond any doubt a squire was made a knight, either by the simple ceremony of the accolade or stroke of the sword, or by the more elaborate ritual used on special occasions such as coronations. This ritual included fasting and prayer, bathing and robing, from which the knights so created were called Knights of the Bath. This name, only denoting originally knights created with special ceremony, was used in a special sense by George I when he founded the Order of the Bath in 1725.

Unlike the peerage, knighthood is not hereditary. It is laid down by law that "the Knight is by creation and not by descent". Confusion often exists with reference to baronets, who are sometimes called hereditary knights. This description is not accurate. The original baronets or bannerets were knights of greater distinction and authority than knights bachelor. In the army they had a more extensive command and led their men under a banner or square flag. The order of baronets, in the modern sense of an heredity title, was created by James I. The fact that this new title did not automatically make its holder a knight was proved by the granting of a privilege that baronets might, if they so wished, receive knighthood.

Today the ceremony of the accolade is simple and dignified. Investitures usually take place in the Throne Room at Buckingham Palace. The recipient of the honour kneels before the Queen who strikes him a light blow on the shoulder with the flat of a drawn sword, saying "Rise", and calling him by his Christian name with "Sir" before it.

In the simplicity there is little to suggest that, of all the countries in Europe in which chivalry flourished, England is the only one where knighthood still exists and where the subject still receives the honour personally at the hands of his Sovereign. In the United Kingdom the orders of chivalry gradually ceased to be fraternities and became marks of royal favour and the means of rewarding distinguished service. There are now eight Orders of Knighthood—the Garter; the Thistle, for Scotland; St. Patrick, for Ireland; the Bath; the Star of India; St. Michael and St. George; the Indian Empire; the Royal Victorian Order, and the Order of the British Empire. The Order of the Garter, one of the

Prime Orders of Christendom, is the most ancient and noble order still existing. The exact date of its foundation by Edward III is uncertain but it may reasonably be considered to date from 1348 when the letters patent were prepared for the Royal Chapel at Windsor, dedicated to St. George, the patron saint of the Order.

The common tradition of its founding is connected with the Countess of Salisbury's garter but the story is dismissed by Heylyn as "a vain and idle romance derogatory both to the founder and the order". The original Companionship consisted of the Sovereign and twenty-five knights and so it remained until 1786 when it was declared that the sons of George III and his successors were eligible even though the chapter was complete. In 1805 a similar provision was made for the lineal descendants of George II, at the same time putting the Prince of Wales into a position of dignity next to the Sovereign by making the holder of this title "a constituent part of the original institution". The privilege of admission was extended to the lineal descendants of George I in 1831. Little is known about the first admission of ladies but it is certain that Queens Consort and the wives of some of the highest nobles were received into the Order in the fourteenth and fifteenth centuries. This precedent was followed when George VI granted Companionship to his consort, Queen Elizabeth, and to his daughter, now Queen Elizabeth II. The motto of the Order is *Honi Soit Qui Mal y Pense* ("Dishonoured be he who thinks ill of it"), and the insignia consist of the Garter, the Collar and George, the Lesser George, and the Star. The ceremony of the Garter Service at St. George's Chapel, Windsor, is marked by great splendour and dignity. Until the reign of Charles II the Sovereign and his knights always walked in procession to this service. The next monarch to do so was George V when in 1912 he revived a custom the pageantry of which has given immense pleasure every time it has been carried out. On these occasions the Military Knights of Windsor take their parts in the ceremonial. This foundation of officers, picturesque in their scarlet uniforms and black silk cocked hats, is a relic of the original establishment of the Order of the Garter. It was then decreed that twenty-four Poor Knights should be supported out of the funds of the Chapel of St. George. Later the number was reduced to thirteen and the name changed to the Military Knights.

The Most Ancient Order of the Thistle, founded by James II in 1687 and dedicated to St. Andrew, had a short initial life. It disappeared with the Revolution of 1688 but was revived by Queen Anne in 1703. Originally it contained only eight knights, in addition to the Sovereign. This number was increased first to twelve and later to sixteen but the Order still has the distinction of limiting itself to the smallest number of companions. Its motto is *Nemo me impune lacessit* ("No one provokes me with impunity"). Its chapel, in St. Giles's Cathedral, Edinburgh, was built in 1909. Here are held the impressive installation services, one of which occurred early in the reign of Elizabeth II. The Queen, wearing the dark green velvet cloak of the Order, the green cap and white ostrich plume, and the golden collar of thistles and sprigs of rue, walked in procession to the Cathedral. Preceding Her Majesty was the splendid group of officials of the Lyon Court—Lord Lyon King of Arms, Heralds, Pursuivants and the Usher of the Green Rod— followed by the thirteen existing knights who that day were to have three added to their number.

The Most Illustrious Order of St. Patrick was founded by George III in 1788. Originally it consisted of the Sovereign, the Lord Lieutenant of Ireland as Grand Master, and fifteen knights companion. The number was increased to twenty-two knights in 1833. The chapel is in St. Patrick's Cathedral, Dublin. Its motto is *Quis Separabit?* ("Who shall separate?").

The Most Honourable Order of the Bath has a confused history. When George I founded the order in 1725 he claimed to be reviving an ancient order supposed to have been created by Henry IV in 1399. But it seems certain that the Knights of the Bath who were created at most coronations from that of Henry IV to that of Charles II were only knights bachelor installed with more splendid ceremony than usual. The order has been enlarged several times and now contains over one thousand knights and companions. Its motto is *Tria juncto in uno* and its services are held in Westminster Abbey. At the inauguration service in 1725, a ceremony of great dignity, the first knights companion were seen in their extraordinary tall white feathered hats.

The fifth and seventh orders are both connected with British service in India. The Most Exalted Order of the Star of India was founded in 1861 and the Most Eminent Order of the Indian Empire in 1878. Both have been several times enlarged, notably in commemoration of Queen Victoria's assumption of the imperial style and title as Empress of India. Between these two ranks the Most Distinguished Order of St. Michael and St. George, founded by the Prince Regent in 1818 "for natives of the Ionian Islands and of the Island of Malta and its dependencies, and for such other subjects of His Majesty as may hold high and confidential situations in the Mediterranean". When Great Britain relinquished the protectorate of the Ionian Islands the Order was reconstituted and extended to permit its honours to be granted to subjects of the Crown holding high and confidential office within the colonial possessions. Its motto is

Auspicium Melioris Devi and its chapel is situated in St. Paul's Cathedral.

The eighth of the orders of knighthood is the Royal Victorian Order, created by Queen Victoria in 1896 as an honour for those who rendered personal services to Her Majesty and her successors on the throne. Its motto is the name of its foundress, *Victoria*.

The ninth order of knighthood is the Most Excellent Order of the British Empire, founded by King George V in 1917, for services rendered to the Empire, whether at home or abroad. It has six grades and is open to both men and women. Its motto is *For God and the Empire*. This order and the Royal Victorian Order are unlike the other seven in being numerically unlimited in membership.

Ranking after the first class of the Order of the Bath comes a great distinction of a different type. This is the Order of Merit, founded by Edward VII on the occasion of his coronation. It is designed as a mark of special honour for eminent men and women without conferring on them a knighthood. Membership is of two kinds, military and civil, and is limited to twenty-four persons. The names of some of the holders of this distinction—Lord Roberts, Lord Kitchener, Lord Jellicoe, Lord Beatty, G. F. Watts, Florence Nightingale, Lord Rutherford, Sir William Bragg and Winston Churchill—are in themselves witnesses that the essential spirit which animated the ancient orders of chivalry is still alive and is capable of finding new expression in a different world. The Order of Merit, placing as it does the highest but most simple mark of honour upon the greatest men and women of our race, is a true expression of the perception of a great king in understanding the minds and hearts of his people.

12. The Monarchy and the People

THESE pages have been concerned with the high formality of British history, distilled in many forms of custom and ceremonial by which the essential spirit of antiquity may yet prove potent in our own day. The forms still exist and have an undeniable vitality, yet they are so much a part of the atmosphere of our lives, the new mingling imperceptibly with the old, that they appear to touch us seldom and even then with a contact so accustomed that we are hardly conscious of their presence. An exception is the coronation, which does not occur so often in a lifetime that any man may fail to recognize its impact, or may pass before its grave ritual unaware that it establishes a unique relationship amongst all those who share in it. Not only those—Sovereign, prelates, nobles, and citizens—who gather in Westminster Abbey, but amongst everyone, thoughtful or thoughtless, mute or acclaiming, to the farthest reaches of the Commonwealth. While these occasions are, by their nature, rare and solemn, there are others when the Monarch and his people seem to take holiday together. These events, when ceremony wears its smile, may not be the great days of our national life, but they are some of the happiest and so some of the most memorable. To think of them calls up a holiday mood, as if we have taken from a drawer an old diary, and, turning the pages, are caught into the atmosphere of days of enjoyment.

Hardly has the year begun before Twelfth Day, old Christmas Day, offers its warm memories, mingling the delights of a homespun festival in medieval England with the glittering splendour of a masque by Ben Jonson and Inigo Jones played at the Stuart Court on Twelfth Night. But before the peasants of Edward I enjoyed their simple revels or the courtiers gathered in their magnificence at Whitehall on the same day four hundred years later, the Sovereign had always celebrated the Feast of the Epiphany, even as it is celebrated today, by the procession to the Chapel Royal at St. James's. Perhaps not exactly as it is celebrated today, because until the time of George III the Monarch went in person with his gifts of gold, frankincense, and myrrh. For nearly two hundred years the offerings have been made on behalf of the Sovereign by Gentlemen-Ushers, attended by Yeomen of the Guard.

On Maundy Thursday, or Holy Thursday, the day before Good Friday, another procession is formed which brings the Monarch close to his people. The Sovereign, or in his absence the Lord High Almoner, goes to Westminster Abbey to distribute Maundy Money to as many poor men and women as the years of his age. The name of the ceremony is probably derived from *Mandatum*, from Christ's words after He had washed the feet of the disciples at the Last Supper, "A new commandment give I unto you". In the Middle Ages the King washed the feet of the poor people and then distributed meat, money, and garments. James II was the last monarch to perform in person the ceremony of washing. William III and his successors delegated this part of the ritual to the Lord High Almoner until 1754 when it was abandoned, leaving only the procession, the service and the presentation of gifts. Money now takes the place of goods. It is carried by a Yeoman of the Guard in red and white purses on a gold dish made for the purpose by Charles II.

With the summer come the ceremonies in the open air. In June is the celebration of the Sovereign's official birthday, with the Trooping the Colour, described in an earlier chapter.

June and July bring the race meetings at Ascot. Ascot Heath was laid out as a race-course by Queen Anne in 1711. The first meeting, on 11th August in that year, was attended by the Queen in a brilliant style which foreshadowed the fashionable splendours of the next two and a half centuries. The Ascot Gold Cup race was instituted by George III in 1807. Six years later Ascot Heath was assigned to the King by the Inclosure Act, to be "kept and continued as a Race Course for the public use at all times as it has usually been". It was George IV, with his faultless sense of display, who initiated the Royal Procession, when, in 1820, he drove on the course up the New Mile in a coach and four with a splendid retinue. The royal carriage procession from the Golden Gates still gives immense pleasure to the thousands who line the course every year.

The royal visits to Scotland usually commence in August and last at least two months. These visits are of an informal nature and much of the State ceremonial is transferred to the Lord High Commissioner to the Church of Scotland while he is in official residence at Holyrood Palace. This dignitary, who is the Sovereign's personal representative, is appointed annually. During his period of residence the Lord High Constable of Scotland attends his functions as if the Sovereign were present in person.

The State Opening of Parliament brightens the dull days of November with the glow of scarlet and blue and the flash of steel and glass as the Sovereign rides in the Irish State

Coach, with an escort of Household Cavalry, from Buckingham Palace to Westminster. A smaller escort, consisting
of a Corporal of Horse and six men, conveys the regalia
from the Tower. This guard is a comparatively recent
precaution. In 1847 the Deputy-Lieutenant of the Tower
protested that the crown was conveyed by three persons
in an ordinary one-horse cab. One of the most impressive
parts of the ceremony of opening Parliament is seen by no
spectators. A dismounted party of the Household Cavalry,
consisting of an officer, two trumpeters, and thirty-six
other ranks dressed in mounted review order, lines the
staircase leading to the robing-rooms. As the Sovereign
goes up they give the Royal Salute and when he passes
from the robing-room into the Royal Gallery the trumpeters
sound a fanfare. The Lords-in-Waiting step back, the doors
are thrown open, and the procession enters the House of
Lords. It is headed by the Heralds in their tabards. The
Sword of State and the crown are borne by the Great Officers.
The Sovereign passes through the chamber, ascends the steps
and takes his seat upon the throne. Around him are assembled the members of both Houses, the Commons having
been summoned by Black Rod to attend at the bar of the
House of Lords. The speech declaring the causes of the
summoning of Parliament, without the reading of which
Parliament cannot proceed to its business, is presented by
the Lord Chancellor to the Sovereign, who either reads it
in person or returns it to the Chancellor requesting him to
read it. At the end of the ceremony, when the procession
has returned to Buckingham Palace, the Field Officer leads
the escort through the arch. The Sovereign stands at the
north door of the Palace as the escort marches past in column
of sections, the royal standard being dipped.

George V and George VI used the intimate means of communication afforded by radio to establish a close relationship with their subjects on Christmas Day. The broadcasts made by the two Kings on Christmas afternoon became a well-loved feature of the holiday celebrations. It is good to know that Queen Elizabeth II, whose broadcast from South Africa on her coming-of-age was so memorable, has carried on this tradition and will broadcast again on her coronation day, when millions of her subjects will be able to see portions of the coronation ceremony itself through the medium of television.

The Sovereign's visits to the City of London are occasions of great splendour, which, as they are attended by processions passing through the main streets of the metropolis, cause great pleasure to vast numbers of spectators. The Lord Mayor, by ancient custom, meets the Sovereign at Temple Bar and delivers to him the City Sword, as to a feudal lord. The sword is returned to him again and he accompanies his monarch into the city, within the boundaries of which he ranks as the first subject in the realm. He has important duties to perform in State ceremonial. At the coronation he carries the Crystal Mace; he is an indispensable member of the Accession Council; in the days when the Coronation Banquet was held in Westminster Hall he was one of several who assisted the Chief Butler in waiting on the King and received a gold cup for his service. A new sovereign is always entertained at luncheon or a banquet by the Lord Mayor in Guildhall, when the superb City plate is used or displayed.

Royal visits to the theatre are usually of a private nature, but State performances are still given at the Royal Opera House, Covent Garden, on the occasion of a coronation or the visit of a foreign sovereign or chief of State. The Yeomen of the Guard are then on duty near the Royal Box.

An interesting and little-known connexion of the Royal Family with the Opera House may be found in the use of members of the Brigade of Guards for walking-on parts in certain opera productions. This practice originated during the reign of Queen Victoria, when, on one of her visits to the opera, the Queen noticed the ragged appearance of members of the chorus who were taking the part of soldiers.

Until the reign of Queen Anne the monarchy exercised a strange and important influence upon the lives of the people through the widespread belief that the English and French kings, alone of all the sovereigns of Christendom, possessed the supernatural power of healing by their touch the disease known as the scrofula or King's Evil. The origin of the superstition may have derived from the miraculous powers of the French Crusader-King, Louis IX, which were thought to have been passed on to the English Royal House by his descendant, Isabella of Valois, consort of Edward II. The Stuart kings usually performed the ceremony in the Banqueting House, Whitehall. Here Evelyn saw Charles II touching the sick and recorded a careful description of the ritual. One of the most famous sufferers from the disease was Samuel Johnson. On the advice of the celebrated physician, Sir John Floyer, Mrs. Johnson brought her son, then aged two years and a half, to London to be touched by Queen Anne. Unfortunately the royal touch did not cure him. About this time people became critical of the practice, associating it with the unpopular doctrine of the divine right of kings. The Hanoverian kings refused to perform the ceremony, which thus died with the last Stuart monarch.

It will be pleasant to draw this chapter and the book to a conclusion with a note on an ancient custom linking the

Sovereign with some of his younger subjects. The boys educated in the Royal Mathematical School of Christ's Hospital claimed the right, from a precedent set in the reign of Charles II, to attend at the Palace on the first Drawing Room in every year. Forty boys, in the early Tudor costume which has earned them the name of Blue Coat Schoolboys, with the President and Treasurer of the foundation, went every year to the Palace to pay their respects to their Sovereign. Because of their numbers six were chosen to enter the Throne Room. There they dropped on their knees and displayed their maps and other exercises for the royal inspection. Within a few weeks of Queen Victoria's accession to the throne the boys secretly determined to present her with an address of congratulation. Unfortunately for their presumptuous but gallant plan a rumour of their intention appeared in a newspaper and steps were taken to prevent "such an irregularity". Happily the boys were not made to suffer as they continued to visit their Queen "in the usual way and upon the usual occasion" until the school left the City.

We close the old diary and put it back in the drawer. Its entries have a nostalgic charm but we cannot linger amongst these fading rose petals. A new Queen is on the throne. We will have a new diary to write up with events as happy and as memorable as any in our history. There will be the old ceremonies, strong with the tradition of centuries; perhaps there will be new ceremonies born of the ever-growing vitality of our Commonwealth of Nations. On all these occasions people will rejoice but will still be conscious of the winds of fate that blow about our island. There will be moments when their thoughts will be with their Sovereign, not only personally in the weight of duties laid on her by her office but also as a representative of the tradition of kingship. The expression of these thoughts is not easy and one would hesitate to say that it is fully achieved in anything as near a habit as the performance of the National Anthem. And yet that habit, now over two hundred years old, is still capable of revealing a sense of continuity in the conception of Monarch and People and in what they mean to each other. It is typical of the almost casual growth of this undemonstrative relationship that, in spite of the intense researches of scholars, no one knows who composed our National Anthem nor with any conviction when it was first sung.

The names of such great English composers as Dr. John Bull and Henry Purcell have been mentioned in connexion with it and it is possible that there was a hymn in honour of the Stuart family that was known to Purcell, but certainty only becomes possible in 1745. On 28th September of that year the news of the defeat of Sir John Cope's army at Prestonpans became known in London and the National Anthem, in a form similar to that in which we know it today, was sung at the Theatres Royal in Drury Lane and Covent Garden. During the next month it was published in the *Gentleman's Magazine*. It was called simply "A Song for Two Voices", and from that spontaneous outburst of popular emotion, caused by the personal danger in which the King stood, with enemies in arms within his own borders, sprang the hymn that we now take almost for granted.

In the year of a new coronation and in many years to come people will seek the consolation and encouragement of their history. These will not be found by knowledge alone but by an exercise of historical imagination such as that which enables the ardours and endurances, the dangers and the hopes to be seen behind the words "God save our gracious Queen".

Index